"... the undisputed king of all the slot books,"
says *The Player* magazine.

SLOT MACHINE

MANIA

DWIGHT E. CREVELT

LOUISE G. CREVELT

GOLLEHON BOOKS
GRAND RAPIDS, MI

Copyright © 1988, 1989
by Gollehon Press, Inc.

ALL RIGHTS RESERVED under international and Pan-American copyright
conventions.

No part of this book may be reproduced or copied in any form or by any means,
including graphic, electronic, mechanical, or information and retrieval systems,
without written permission of the publisher.

Newspaper or magazine writers may quote brief passages for inclusion in a
feature article or review, provided full credit is given.

MANUFACTURED IN THE UNITED STATES OF AMERICA

Library of Congress Catalog Card Number: 87-83322

ISBN 0-914839-13-6
(International Standard Book Number)

Photo of author, courtesy of Gemini Studios.

Contents

The authors wish to express appreciation to those who consented to interviews or shared their knowledge, experiences, and material for this work including:

International Game Technology and Tom Potters, Director of Product Information Services

Russ Scott, Casino Host, Maxim Hotel

John Stroup, Slot Manager,
Las Vegas Flamingo Hilton

Dan Reaser, Chief Deputy Attorney General for the Gaming Commission of the State of Nevada

Debbie Crumm, Public Relations Department, Golden Nugget Casino/Hotel

Anonymous members, past and present, of the Gaming Control Board, the manufacturing industry, the casinos, and the slot cheating community.

Special thanks to John Gollehon for his patience in waiting for us to get it all together.

Foreword

Don't ask me the month, or the year, but it was a Sunday. . .and when we got up that morning our first thoughts were to do something to get us out of the casino. We had been in Las Vegas for a few days and although I consider myself a good player, I was on the short end of about two grand in markers. Indeed, we decided not to even eat in the casino, but to eat on the way. To where? No difference. Just as long as where we were going, there weren't any blackjack tables, or craps tables or slot machines, or even a sports book. "Just get me the hell out of here!" Ever had the same feeling?

It's funny. I've written nearly a dozen books about

gambling, published several others, and most people who know me wonder why I don't live in Las Vegas. With that kind of expertise, they surmise, why doesn't he make his living at the tables?

I'm not Jimmy Connors who can beat the pants off most tennis players, and I'm not Jack Nicklaus or a beginning pro out looking for a foursome and a $20 Nassau. These guys *are* experts, and their games can support them. But in the games in the casino, there are no experts. It makes no difference how well you know the rules, or the skills (if there are any), or the stories, or the casino managers, or anything. Even at blackjack today, I don't know of any casino that won't welcome any player, expert or not. You can't beat the odds with expertise! Am I an expert? Well, I know the games as well as anyone, but I can't make the dice jump off a seven; I can't expertly throw the dice like Joe Montana throws a football; and I can't magically make the cards come out of the shoe to give me blackjacks. I don't have a photographic memory, so I can't count down a 6-deck shoe that's been cut a third of the way.

Like I said earlier, "Just get me out of the casino, away from the tables, to the mountains, Lake Mead, the Nevada Test Site...anywhere!"

Valet brought us our car, and we headed out towards Hoover Dam and Lake Mead where every other stereotyped "tourist" heads when the hundred dollar bills thin out in his wallet. We stopped for a cheap breakfast, an antique shop or two along the way, and then, almost there, we saw a turn-off for Laughlin. Laughlin? I had heard about the town and how pretty the Colorado River is down there, and how picturesque the drive is through the desert. So why not.

After what seemed like four or five hours, and a lot of

desert (a lot more than I really wanted to see), we finally got there and gee what a thrill it was. Five casinos or so stuck along the river like casinos in Las Vegas, casinos in Reno, casinos in Lake Tahoe, casinos in Atlantic City. Inside, there were slot machines, and more slot machines... slot machines all over the place! The casinos all looked alike — noisy, low ceilings, players bumping into one another, aisles that were so crowded you wondered how the local fire marshall could approve the place. But I guarantee you, if anyone had to empty the place in a hurry, you would need your boy scout compass to get out of the maze... or a map.

Let's see. Go down the first aisle of quarter poker machines, turn left at the big million dollar display board, head straight past all the nickel machines, hang a right at the one dollar 3-reelers, then right again at the change-booth, look for the "Big Bertha" machine, and you're at the door. But this is the door to the gift shops! Where's the main entrance?!

It always amazes me how the guys who designed these places could actually find room for gift shops, restaurants, and restrooms. Now I hear that some casinos are thinking about putting slot machines in the restrooms! If you thought your wife took a long time to "powder her nose," with slots in there we could be talking hours and hours!

After leaving the casino, we noticed that the parking lots were full. One bus after another. Later, we learned that most of the people who take the buses to Laughlin are from retirement communities in Arizona. So many of our senior citizens living in Arizona have little to do except enjoy the sun, the desert, and Laughlin's thousands of slot machines. My guess is when the Social Security checks come in the mail on Tuesday, Laughlin's hopping on Wednesday!

Make no mistake, Laughlin is in Nevada, barely. But across the river *is* Arizona; and Laughlin, for all intents and purposes, is Arizona's legalized gambling. Laughlin is in Arizona if you go by all the license plates on the cars in the parking lots.

After we finally found our own car (why is it rental cars all look alike?), we couldn't help but notice the pretty mountains nearby. My 10-year-old son, Johnny, loves to climb the mountains and look for rocks. He's not ready for Mt. Everest, but he really enjoys climbing mountains. I don't. So I tell him the mountains are full of rattlesnakes but he hasn't bought that yet. I'm tempted to invest in one of those rubber snakes, and put an end to all this foolishness.

Anyhow, we went mountain climbing and looking for rocks (you know, the blue, red, or green rocks, not the plain brown and gray ones). After we loaded up our trunk with half of Laughlin's rocks, we left town, wondering about two things: why did we come here in the first place, and why is the car riding so low?

On the way back to Las Vegas, I told my wife that these people playing slot machines are all crazy. They're maniacs! Slot machine maniacs! Someone has to do a book about this phenomenon, and the title was too easy. *Slot Machine Mania!*

Not a book about old machines. Old machines are old news. And no pretty pictures of machines. If we included pictures of today's most popular machines, sure enough, three days after the book came out, the machines would be obsolete. What I really wanted was a book not so much about the machines themselves, but about the people who play them, and the mania that has been let loose from these crazy contraptions.

You'll enjoy this book. I promise you. And if you decide to play the machines, even if you never have before, promise *me* that you'll only take with you the money you can afford to lose. Because you probably will. And if that doesn't work, walk out of the casino and head straight for the mountains. Nevada has lots of pretty mountains covered with lots of pretty rocks. Mountain climbing and rock hunting are free!

But don't try this in Atlantic City. It only works in Nevada. In Atlantic City, you can't even find sea shells anymore. I wonder if they have rattlesnakes.

Have fun!

John Gollehon

This book is dedicated to Matthew Henry Crevelt, born appropriately on April 21, 1987, weight 7 pounds 11 ounces, height 21 inches and to his mother Jean Anne Crevelt. Also, to his brother William Michael, sister Michelle Anne, and grandfather James R. Crevelt for their patience and understanding.

INTRODUCTION

"Delightful Madness," "Pure Insanity," "Hypnotic Fascination," "Glittering Gluttony," "Sensual Greed," "Gaudy Delight," "Lurid Luck," "Charming Chance," "Ecstatic Folly," "Foolish Fantasy," "Crazy Clunking," "Hopeless Hope," and "Ultimate Urge." These are a few of the alliterative and contradictory epithets we've heard to describe this phenomenon we call "Slot Machine Mania."

We call it "Mania" because slot playing makes no logical sense, but it has captured the imagination and attention of pleasure-seekers everywhere. It is one of the most popular and lucrative forms of gambling in the world. Popular with players and lucrative for the gaming industry, that is.

Walking through a busy casino and observing people chucking coins into slots and pulling handles as fast as they can while whistles blow, bells ring, music plays, and winners scream with delight must be the modern equivalent to a Roman orgy. It surpasses the excitement of being a mere spectator at the Olympics or the Super Bowl. Why? Because everyone can play! And it's so easy!

Easy? Of course! You don't have to know anything to be able to participate. You can easily become caught up in the player's excitement and find it virtually impossible to resist "trying your luck." You can easily be tempted to try for a bigger win after you've won a few coins, especially if the next machine is spitting out coins by the bucketful. It's easy to become mesmerized by spinning wheels, flashing lights, and the challenge of playing cards dealt so quickly you can't put in coins fast enough to keep up with the machine. It's easy to keep reaching into the tray of dropped coins and put them right back into the hungry machine. It's easy to reach into your purse or wallet for more bills when the tray is empty and you still haven't hit the jackpot and its promise of instant riches. It's easy to become hooked on playing slots because it's "only a game."

Only a game? True. But it takes real money to play. And the consequences of losing are real too. Why then do so many educated, intelligent, astute and otherwise cautious people exhibit such illogical behavior? Perhaps we should ask Mr. Spock!

We will try to answer these questions you have always wanted to ask and dispel the myths and misconceptions fostered by so-called "experts." We have tried to analyze this maniacal phenomenon and record for everyone the in's and out's of this fascinating and sometimes painful pleasure.

Our intention is not to encourage slot playing as a way to earn a living, nor do we encourage you to play if you have the slightest reservation. Our purpose is solely to give you more knowledge about slots and slot playing as a recreational pastime. We hope that after reading this book you will experience more "highs" than "lows," and have fun along the way.

Having fun is at least half the reason most players pull the handles. The other half is, of course, the chance of winning. Trying to overcome ridiculous odds. That's how otherwise ordinary people become folk heroes. They accomplish the seemingly impossible feat by winning in the face of overwhelming odds. Everyone dreams of being some kind of hero or heroine. So, they challenge the odds. Sometimes foolishly, sometimes armed with as much knowledge and ammunition against their opponents as possible to compensate for the odds against them. It's the universal dream, *to win the prize!*

With slot machine playing as with any other gamble, the soundest advice to give any player is, "PLAY SMART!" Reducing the odds against you, increasing your chances of winning, minimizing your losses—it's the same thing here. You have no control over the odds programmed into a given machine or the amount of payout posted in a given pay table on the machine. But you can at least look for the best pay tables with certain types of machines that we'll learn about later.

You don't have to spend years "working" the slots to learn to play smart. But you would be surprised how many players have spent years and thousands of dollars without learning some basic disciplines—rules that may not always help you win but may help you win the most you can when you are "lucky" enough to hit the big one. What we are talking about here is using plain, common sense. A trait that's in short supply among most slot players. Of course, you will never completely eliminate the element of "chance" or "luck." But you can at least minimize your exposure and try the "hit and run" approach that we'll talk about later. We want you to learn how to "quit winners."

An important step is to learn as much as you can about the game you intend to play and about your opponent. Yes, your opponent. With slot playing, your opponent is not the casino, not the shift boss, not even the slot manager. It's the SLOT MACHINE. Once you learn what makes that machine tick, or click, or better yet, clink with coins in the tray, you can learn to play more effectively.

Some basic rules or strategies to follow are described in detail in other chapters. But let us briefly outline what you should learn to become an informed and cautious slot machine player. And let's emphasize "player." Always consider yourself a game player, out for entertainment, and you're less likely to become a "victim" or "addict."

Playing the Odds

The main reason to study the odds and percentages of slot machines is so you can stop worrying about them. Unless you intend to become a professional gambler, a sports handicapper, a casino owner, or an author on mathematical probabilities, an in-depth study of odds

won't help you much in playing slots, and it can ruin your
fun.

Remember that the odds are always in favor of the
casino. If not, there wouldn't be so many machines and
they wouldn't be constantly expanding throughout the
casinos. *Every slot machine you find is built to take most
or all of your money if you let it.*

Some casinos may advertise that they have the loosest
slots or that they return up to 97.5% or 98%. One Las
Vegas casino boasts up to 101% returned. Don't be fooled.
The casinos are not settling for a take of 2 or 2.5 percent
and they're not guaranteeing you a penny's worth of profit for every dollar you play.

The slot machines in every casino will be programmed
with a variety of percentages and you'll never know what
the percentage of return is except in rare places where a
few machines actually have a percentage posted.

In Nevada, even the state regulatory agencies have not
decreed that machines have a minimum percentage of
return. Consequently, depending on the owner's preference, his business sense, the amount of competition, and
his sense of fairness to his customers, machines may be
programmed with percentages anywhere between 50 and
99.5 (101?) percent. However, *most of them we believe are
in the 85 to 97 percent range.*

On the other hand in Atlantic City, the regulatory agencies ruled that 83% is the minimum allowable. People are
standing in line at the casinos to play a machine. With that
kind of action, you can probably draw your own conclu-
sions on what the percentages are for most of the machines
there. Suffice to say that the casinos don't really need to
be generous. There are cheaper ways to attract players to

the casinos and we have described some of them in the section on special promotions.

Plus, you'll enjoy the chapter on *Machines and How They Work*. You'll learn:

1. How to tell the difference between the mechanicals, electro-mechanicals and the microprocessor controlled types.

2. How to determine what you can win before you put in your coins by carefully reading the award glass or the payout table on the video screen.

3. How to determine how many coins you must play to win the highest jackpot if that is your goal.

4. The difference between single pay lines and multiple pay lines types as well as option payout machines.

5. The differences between straight payouts and progressive jackpots and the resulting reduction in "small wins."

6. Decide between straight slot machines or the games that require some thought or skill. You may want to try both at first to see which you prefer for extended play.

Decide Where To Play

If you live in Nevada, you probably already know that there is no other place with as wide a variety of casinos or other places with slot machines. If you live in the East, the nearest spot is Atlantic City. If you live anywhere else, the chapter on *Where to Play* will give you an overview of the choices for atmosphere and types of machines and jackpots by location. It will also list other attractions if gambling is not the sole purpose for your trip.

If slots are your target, the chapter will steer you to what we hope is the most likely spot to win the most for your money.

Don't Be Pre-Deceived

Forget most of what you've heard from other occasional players who have either "won big" or "lost their shirts." They may think they're experts either way.

Don't be discouraged by the losers who will swear that all the casinos are crooked and all the machines are rigged to cheat you. The sections on regulatory controls should reassure you somewhat of the safeguards to protect players. The chapter on cheating should put that facet in proper perspective. Likewise, the chapters on *Misconceptions* and *Superstitions*, we hope, will dispel the many myths that have been circulated on ineffective systems and ways of manipulating or controlling the machines.

Play with Self-Discipline

Maintaining self-control is difficult but most important as we mention time and time again in this book. A steady diet of slot playing has broken down the will power of some people we know who quit smoking cold turkey, lost weight on strict diets or showed remarkable persistence in accomplishing other goals.

A few ways to maintain self-discipline should be read and even memorized to serve as ready reminders. Program your mind, your conscience or your sensibility to recall them each time you plan to play for an hour or more.

1. Don't be so anxious to play that you grab the first machine open, even if you recognize it as one you won on

before or saw someone else hit. Take your time and look for the machine you can easily understand, has the right coin value for your budget, and that you feel comfortable with.

2. If a machine you are playing isn't paying, leave it before you put too much into it. Common sense? You would be surprised how many players act as if they are "chained" to a cold machine!

3. Don't take money into a casino that you can't afford to lose. Read the chapter on *Money Management* and make it work for you.

4. Always play with a positive attitude. If you're grumpy, you'll probably get angry. If you're having bad luck, go home and watch TV or read a good book. If you want to stay in the casino in spite of your luck, just watch other people play. It's great therapy and it won't cost you a penny!

5. Don't drink while playing. Booze impairs your judgment and weakens your will-power.

6. Play your hunch if you really have one. We don't know why, but intuition can sometimes be your best guide. If you tell yourself it's time to stop playing or to change machines, it usually is.

7 thru 70. Quit when you're ahead.

Some good indicators that you are losing control are:

1. Your positive attitude is turning to a negative one.

2. You start to feel "guilty" about the amount of money you've lost.

3. You get desperate to win, to recoup your losses.

4. You have played back all the coins the machine dropped and think it's going to start paying you again.

5. You start lying to yourself such as, "I'd spend more

than this buying new clothes I don't need and it isn't nearly as much fun.''

6. You laugh and joke with fellow players about how much money you've lost as if it didn't matter.

7. You can't quit when you're ahead.

Look for these signs and learn to respond to them.

Be Selective

Decide which machines are most appropriate to your interests, your bankroll, and your expectations. There's something for everyone in the slot arena from penny slots for long-lasting fun at a minor investment, to $100 slots for a high-roller thrill at a substantial risk, and all the stages in between.

Look for the machines that fit your style and have fun, but don't be tempted to disaster when you see someone else win on a machine that is beyond your means.

If you typically go home a loser like most everyone else, then this book is for you. Maybe it can help. Maybe not. But one thing is for sure. You can't take your favorite slot machine home with you and play it, but you *can* take what we hope becomes your favorite book home with you and read it, and read it again.

Maybe, just maybe, you'll realize that simply playing the machines, and having the opportunity to win, is the real fun. We're betting that's the reason why right now you can't wait to tie down your favorite machine and sit a spell. If you realize that, then you're not a loser. No sir! You're the biggest winner of them all!

May you have the time of your life!

CHAPTER 1

Machines and How They Work

You don't really want to know how to build a slot machine so rest assured this chapter won't detail mechanics of their innards. We have described the main features of the older mechanical and electro-mechanical units under the brief history of manufacturers in a later chapter. Since their use is now practically history, we'll concentrate on their successors, the microprocessor machines. We'll learn how they operate and how they are programmed to expand the odds, making possible the super jackpots while generating big revenue for the casinos.

Mechanical Machines

These machines earned the nickname, "one armed bandits." Their "arms" or handles were such an integral part of the play that the new microprocessor machines still have handles to pull although the handle has absolutely no function except to activate the machine, which could also be done by pushing a button. Some slots actually have both buttons and handles.

Actual spinning reels was the other feature that fascinated players. Recent machines with 13″ video screens displaying the simulation of spinning reels did not impress many slot players. In fact, most players were cynical of their design. Consequently, manufacturers are again making machines with real "reels" but which are controlled by stepper motors, that are in turn controlled by the microprocessor program.

The highest jackpots of true mechanical machines rarely exceeded $25 and the automatic payout was small. Large wins were paid by an attendant.

So don't be fooled on your first visit to a casino. Old mechanicals have a different "feel" to the handle although manufacturers have tried to simulate it with the new handles. The sound of gears meshing and the clicks of metal as the reels "stop" or bounce are noticeable on mechanicals. The sound is definitely different from the "built-in" noise of chirps, whirrs, and music in the micros.

Electro-Mechanical Machines

The electro-mechanical slots began replacing the

mechanicals in the late 50's, 60's and early 70's. Now they are rapidly disappearing from the scene to make way for the microprocessor controlled units.

This group of slots included refinements such as multiple coin play, multiple pay lines, "buy-a-pay" features, progressive jackpots and more anti-cheating safeguards. Despite these safeguards there are approximately 120 different ways to cheat an old electro-mechanical machine, especially if it is not adjusted properly.

Electrically powered enhancements were coin meters, flashing lights, noise makers and hoppers that held more coins than the old coin tubes and could pay out larger amounts automatically. However, verifying, paying, and tracking large jackpots was still done manually. If a machine paid out frequent small wins and had to have its hopper refilled more than two or three times in a short period, the casino would shut it down to check for a possible malfunction or presence of cheating devices. Players with a "hot" machine got pretty "hot under the collar" when their machine was shut down.

Many of the old electro-mechanicals still in use may look the same but most have been converted into microprocessor units. **So don't assume "easy" odds by the way a machine looks. It might look "old" on the outside but have the most modern computer design on the *inside!*** Summit Coin was one of the first manufacturers to produce a kit used to convert these machines. Converting them was more economical than purchasing the micros.

Electronic Machines

Electronic machines were transitional units and short-lived. They used solid state technology at a time when casinos and the public were still skeptical of rapidly developing electronic devices. Only the most forward-looking casinos would install a few of them.

In 1974, Gamex Industries—where this author began his association with gaming—developed one of the first totally electronic slot machines. A number of them were installed at Caesars Palace and received more play than the traditional machines. They also added much color and light to the normally dim and subdued atmosphere of Caesars.

But the solid state technology was rapidly replaced by the more reliable microprocessors, so electronic machines virtually disappeared. Manufacturers began to compete with each other to develop the best microprocessor-controlled slot.

Microprocessor-Controlled Machines

Microprocessors, often called "chips," are miniature computers which work in conjunction with other "chips" or integrated circuits (IC's) to control all parts of the machine, from the lights behind the award and logo glasses, to the coin meters, the automatic hopper, video screen and symbols displayed, and even the "reels" in the newest look of slots that simulate the old mechanicals. One or a series of these chips hold the programmed memory that performs all the intricate functions as well as generate the win-loss symbols important to the player.

It is impossible to systematically play a microprocessor-controlled machine, provided it is properly programmed. And it is almost impossible to cheat one unless the memory chip is substituted.

The program is one thing that the gaming control board checks very carefully. They check the algorithms and the method used to calculate or select the random numbers, examining it mathematically, theoretically, and empirically, to make sure the machine performs as it is supposed to and will not cheat the player. Put simply, an algorithm is a formula or sequence of instructions for a task. In the slot machine program, it is a mathematical formula that determines how the number or set of numbers is to be selected and translated into a specific combination and arrangement of symbols to be displayed on the video screen or on the reels.

An important part of the program is the random number generator (RNG). Have you ever heard of a perpetual motion machine? Have you ever watched bees storing honey in a beehive? The frenzied activity never stops until the bees are dead.

Likewise, the microprocessor containing the program and the RNG never stops unless the power is cut off. Every millisecond the RNG selects a random number from a sequence within a given range. Most machines use a 32 bit RNG, which means it will generate a value somewhere between 0 and 4,294,967,296 (exponentially 2 to the 32nd). We will round off the number to 4 billion for discussion purposes. Theoretically, it should select each number in that range at least once before repeating a number, but that is not necessarily true. Within that range of numbers, a specific number or combination of three, four or more numbers is translated into a specific set of symbols. The microprocessor looks somewhat like a fat centipede which ostensibly sits there tapping its little feet until someone inserts a coin to play the machine. But that little "critter" is never quiet. While tapping its feet, it is executing millions

of programmed instructions included in its "memory"
such as checking paytables or making sure no one is
tampering with the hopper, the reels, the door, or other
parts of the machine. It checks and meters coins in, coins
paid, and coins to the drop box and stores that information in the memory. Meanwhile it's waiting for a player.

Player Instigated Action

All modern (computerized) machines operate on what
is called "Player Instigated Action." (We have included
the acronyn "PIA" for brevity in this explanation. It is
not a common one heard in gaming jargon.) PIA may occur at various times, depending on how the machine is programmed. It may differ with the machine and the manufacturer. PIA could occur at the moment the coin is inserted, accepted and/or registered on the meter, at the instant the player pulls the handle or pushes the button for
"deal," or some specific millisecond after the player does
one of these things. It's all in the program.

When PIA occurs, it's like a "stage cue" or a "curtain
call" to the centipede to go into his "fancy dance" of
selecting the symbols for the machine to play. It accesses
the RNG to tap the treasure stored in that beehive, either
honey (winning symbols) or beeswax (losing symbols).
When PIA occurs, the mathematical formula in the program tells the RNG to select a number or group of numbers
which will correspond to a specific set of symbols. Sometimes the RNG is accessed several times for the combination of symbols on a single play.

If you "knew" at a given millisecond what set of symbols the RNG would display, you still could not

systematically play the machine to display those symbols. Several factors prevent systematic play to "call out" a given set of symbols. First of all, it is literally impossible to know at a given millisecond what symbols the RNG will choose, since the choice is "random," meaning that there is no predetermined sequence of choices. Second, even if you knew the exact millisecond that the winning symbols are supposed to appear, the human reaction time is too slow to play the machine fast enough to freeze that set of symbols. For instance, the average person has a 50 to 350 millisecond reaction time, and mechanical and electrical delays in the machine can vary from 16 to 50 milliseconds between plays. Consequently, there are from 66 to 400 different combinations that can occur during that time over which you have no control.

So much for worrying about another player winning "your" jackpot by playing "your" machine. Now, you can see that if someone else wins a jackpot on the next pull of the machine you had been playing, the RNG determined the timing of the jackpot, not the fact that the jackpot came on the next pull. Even if you had continued playing the machine, you most likely would not have won the jackpot. It's all a question of RNG timing in milliseconds, not the sequence of handle pulls. Surprised?

Basic Machine Configurations

The three basic configurations of slot machines are Multipliers, Multiple Line and Buy-Your-Pay. They are all multiple coin machines. Multiple coin machines are the only type currently manufactured. Single coin, single line machines are obsolete. Although you may find some of these old machines around, they will soon join the antiques. They no longer carry their weight on the casino floor. The MGM Grand in Las Vegas (now Bally's) was the first casino to open with 100% multiple coin machines. The casino experts all said they were crazy. Kirk Kerkorian (the owner) laughed all the way to the bank.

"Multipliers" are those machines that allow you to increase your winnings proportionately by playing multiple coins. Some have an additional incentive jackpot award for playing the maximum coins. Most common multipliers are 2, 3, 4, and 5-coin types although some are found which require 8, 9, and even 10 coins for the incentive award. Generally, multipliers have single pay lines.

CAUTION: ALWAYS MAKE SURE THAT THE APPROPRIATE *SECTIONS* OF THE PAYOUT TABLE ARE LIT BEFORE YOU PULL THE HANDLE. IF THEY'RE NOT, YOU LOSE, EVEN IF YOU ACTUALLY PLAYED THE RIGHT NUMBER OF COINS.

"Multiple line" machines pay small wins and jackpots on more than a single line. Most common are 3-line or 5-line criss-cross types. But in a few you will find as many as 8 lines. Multiple line machines require a coin to be played for every payout line. A space beside each line and also on the award glass of the machine should light up when you insert the appropriate coins to indicate that it is being played and will pay if hit. Most machines have the largest jackpot paid on the highest numbered line. If you don't insert enough coins to light up that line, you won't win the jackpot if it hits.

CAUTION: ALWAYS MAKE SURE THAT THE *LINES* ARE LIT BEFORE YOU PULL THE HANDLE. IF THEY'RE NOT, YOU LOSE, EVEN IF YOU

ACTUALLY PLAYED THE RIGHT NUMBER OF COINS.

"Buy-Your-Pay" machines have a single payout line. They not only require the maximum coins to be played to win the top jackpot, they require a specific number of coins to be inserted to win the smaller payouts. For instance, a 3-coin machine will pay cherries only on the first coin. To win on oranges, or plums you must insert the second coin. For the jackpot on Bars or 7's you have to insert the third coin. There are 2, 3 or 4-coin types with varying types of symbols scattered among the other multipliers and multiple line types.

Watch out for these machines. They've caused unwary players to miss the big win more than any other type. They ought to be called "Buy-Your-Loss" or "Lose Your Pay" machines.

REMEMBER — ALWAYS PLAY THE MAXIMUM NUMBER OF COINS ON THESE MONSTERS. IF YOU DON'T, YOU MIGHT JUST AS WELL HAND THE CASINO YOUR CASH WHEN YOU WALK IN AND SAVE YOURSELF THE TIME AND EFFORT OF PULLING THE HANDLES.

Megabucks

As the name suggests, this super slot by IGT is the *piece de resistance* for slot players.

At 12:24 p.m. on February 1, 1987, Terry Williams of Los Gatos, California hit the first MegaBuck jackpot for $4,988,842.14, at Harrah's Reno. He had only invested $47.00. That's a return of over $106,528 for every dollar! Williams, a 44 year old marriage counselor by day and an electronics technician by night, had intended to go skiing, but a pulled muscle in his back kept him off the slopes. He had played a quarter progressive with a $180,000 jackpot and had stopped to go for a walk. On his return, he stopped at the MEGABUCKS machine and had played for less than 90 minutes before lining up the four sevens. He said that his tray kept filling up with minor payouts so he kept playing. His trip from the San Francisco Bay area to Reno was the first in three years.

The jackpot will be paid in ten annual installments of $499,000 each. Of course, Terry must give Uncle Sam his share for income taxes, but he shouldn't need to continue working day and night. He should now have time to ski and play to his heart's content.

Prior to Williams' win, the largest slot machine jackpot ever hit was for $3 million at Harrah's Tahoe in June 1986 which was at that time the record jackpot for one casino.

Terry Williams visited Reno again to celebrate the anniversary of his Megabucks win and to try to repeat his luck, but the fates had decreed otherwise.

Just as we were finishing this manuscript, MEGABUCKS was hit again for the largest slot jackpot ever. Cammie J. Brewer, 61, of Reno, Nevada went to the Cal Neva Club for their 99-cent breakfast. He eats breakfast there every Sunday with his 81 year-old father-in-law. After playing about $20, Brewer lined up the four sevens for a $6,814,823 jackpot. Wonder if this got him out of the dog house with his wife, since it was Valentine's Day and he had forgotten to get her a present for the first time in 26 years? His largest previous win after 25 years of playing slots was $650.

After Brewer's win, the State Gaming Control Board

inspected the computer chips and the film of the event to make sure it was a legitimate jackpot.

The Megabucks jackpot reached the $6.8 million plus mark approximately one year after it was first hit for $4.9 million. It automatically reset at $1.9 million and is progressing rapidly in the 52 casinos throughout the state. It could hit again at anytime.

MEGABUCKS was introduced on March 6, 1986 with banks of progressive dollar machines in nine casinos, and now totals over 52 installations. The jackpot started at $1 million and grew to almost $5 million in less than one year before it was hit for the first time. An average of $2.25 million weekly is played through the system with the jackpot climbing at the rate of $65,000 to $110,000 each week.

The first MEGABUCKS machines were all microprocessor controlled, 4-reel video machines with a 3-coin, 3-line payout configuration. Lining up four sevens on the first line with $1 played paid $5,000. Four sevens on the second line with $2 bet paid $10,000. The $3 bet covered all three lines and the progressive jackpot was for the four sevens on the third line. The progressive jackpot never drops below $1 million. After it was hit by Williams, the secondary meter automatically reset it at $1.9 million.

MEGABUCKS was first introduced to rival the vast popularity of lotteries in California and other states. In fact, several states including Massachusetts and Oregon have lotteries referred to as "megabucks." Consequently, *the promotional advertising of a statewide slot progressive caused many people to think it was sponsored by the state of Nevada. However, it is entirely owned and operated by the manufacturer, International Game Technology.* IGT produces, installs, and maintains the system, including the machines, display meters, computers, and telephone lines. Further, it handles all administration, advertising and liability for the jackpot payout. All the casinos have to do is rake in their percentage. In essence, MEGABUCKS is handled like IGT's other "slot" routes but with a great deal more promotion.

At an International Gaming Conference recently, IGT unveiled its new MEGABUCKS machine. This new *reel* machine has replaced all the *video* machines. Although the controls are still microprocessors, the machine actually has mechanical spinning reels. Further innovations were the addition of the "MULTI-MINI" jackpot programmed to pay several thousand dollars approximately every two or three days somewhere in the state, depending on the frequency of play. The percentage of the amount played is divided between the major jackpot, the secondary (invisible) meter for reset when the major jackpot is hit, and the MULTI-MINI jackpot.

Within eight days after the reconfiguration to the reel machines, the MULTI-MINI jackpot had been hit about six times. Theoretically, the large jackpot should hit every four or five months and range from $2 to $3 million. On a busy Saturday night the big jackpot increases a dollar about every three seconds. In one recent month's time, Megabucks had paid over $800,000 to 141 players in Mini-jackpots.

As of this writing, the major casinos that have banks of MEGABUCKS machines are:

LAS VEGAS
  California
  Fremont
  Lady Luck

Del Webb's Mint
Fitz
El Cortez
The Golden Gate
Sam's Town
Barbary Coast
Bourbon Street
Stardust
Vegas World
Marina
Tropicana, The Island
Paddlewheel
Landmark

RENO/SPARKS
Harrah's Reno
Comstock Hotel-Casino
Karl's Silver Club
Club Cal-Neva
Fitzgerald's
Boomtown
Eldorado Hotel/Casino
Eddie's Fabulous Fifties
Old Reno Casino
The Sands Regency

OTHERS
Red Lion Inn & Casino, Elko
Red Garter, Wendover
Fallon Nugget, Fallon
Fallon Bonanza, Fallon
Cactus Pete's, Jackpot
Carson Valley Inn, Minden

Gold Strike Inn, Jean
Whiskey Pete's, Jean
Casino West, Yerington
Parker's Model T Casino, Winnemucca
Winner's Inn Hotel/Casino, Winnemucca

STATELINE (South Lake Tahoe)

Harrah's Lake Tahoe
Harvey's Resort
Del Webb's High Sierra
John's Tahoe Nugget
Bill's Lake Tahoe Casino
Lakeside Inn & Casino

CRYSTAL BAY (North Lake Tahoe)

Cal Neva Lodge
Tahoe Biltmore

LAUGHLIN

Sam's Town Gold River
Del Webb's Nevada Club
Don Laughlin's Riverside Resort

CARSON CITY

Cactus Jack's Senator Club
Carson City Nugget
Mother Lode
Ormsby House

One of the main reasons that IGT developed Megabucks was to give the smaller casinos an opportunity to offer their patrons a multi-million dollar jackpot with no risk.

Besides the $5 million jackpot hit by Williams, in

approximately one year after its introduction, Megabucks paid out $110 million in smaller wins.

IGT has obtained approval for a MEGABUCKS system for Atlantic City and is installing a modified version on the island of Macao.

Other High Roller Slots

Recently, Caesars Palace installed three machines that accept only $100 tokens. The top payoff of $100,000 requires a bet of two coins. Ron Dowell of California was one of the first to play the machine. "It feels just like playing a nickel machine," he said. That's a pretty big nickel! He won $500 and kept playing until he lost it.

The machines are manufactured by Universal Distributing of Nevada, and accept only coins specially minted with 10-carat gold centers and silver borders. Mike Moore, casino manager of Caesars, stated that they installed the machines because of popular demand. Do we need any more proof that slot machines are no longer considered the "poor boy's" game?

The Golden Nugget also has a bank of $5.00 slots with a top jackpot of $5 million dollars when you line up four "Golden Nuggets" on the center line of a 3-line, 3-coin machine. That's $15.00 per handle pull when you play. Yes, we are really into the era of slot "high rollers," or maybe we should call them "high reelers."

All-Win Progressives

This type of progressive includes a bank of machines and a display of two jackpots, one large and one smaller, each increasing with play until they reach a predetermined limit if not hit before. It also displays the number of machines in the bank (i.e. 1 thru 16.) Each number lights up when it is being played and stays lit (eligible) for a predetermined amount of time. If a player hits the winning combination, he wins the big one. All other players whose numbers are lit, share the smaller jackpot. When you play an ALL WIN machine, make sure your play is fast enough to keep your number lit at all times. This is extremely important if you play more than one machine. IGT is marketing this concept overseas but is not promoting it very much here in the States. We saw one of these in operation at the El Cortez with a bank of about 16 Keno machines. The top jackpot is $150,000. The smaller shared jackpot is $50,000. The ALL WIN progressive feature is used with all types of machines.

Big Berthas

These huge machines are primarily attractions placed near the casino's front door to lure players inside. They are generally the same as other machines, just bigger and slower. Typically their payouts are not comparable to their bulk.

The Four Queens in downtown Las Vegas boasts the largest slot machine in the world called "The Queen's Machine" which pays a "Queen's Ransom." It contains eight reels and pays on three lines. One, two or three dollars may be played, buying one, two or three pay lines. This machine is designed for multiple players. One to six players sit in "thrones," made of red velvet high back wing chairs. In front of each, a table console includes a coin slot, video winnings display and winner's tray. A "Queen" (change girl) wearing red velvet and golden gown and a gold and jewel encrusted crown pulls the handle of the giant machine after all players have inserted their coins. The standard payout is for cherries, plums, oranges, watermelons, bars and queens. The giant jackpot is a $300,000 aggregate payout for eight queens on the third line. If two cherries show on any of the three lines on either the left or right sides, each player wins five dollars. However, the word "aggregate" is a bummer. If six people are playing when the eight queens line up on the jackpot line, the $300,000 is split six ways. If only one man is playing, he gets the whole pot.

NOTE: ALWAYS WATCH FOR GIANT JACKPOTS WHICH ARE ADVERTISED WITH "AGGREGATE" LIMITS. YOU MAY HAVE TO SPLIT WITH ONE OR MORE PLAYERS WHO HIT AT THE SAME TIME YOU DO.

Another disadvantage to this biggest of the Berthas is that it is so slow. We watched the machine for an hour and it takes approximately 22 seconds for all eight reels to stop after the handle pull. On a 3-reel machine, a spin normally takes approximately six seconds. On a 4-reeler approximately seven seconds. During that hour it hit three oranges twice and three plums once at a payout of $10 each. It hit two cherries once for $5 and a single cherry about eight times for $2 each. The only other hit was five bars for $200. No watermelons hit, nor did the queens, the symbol with the largest payout. Frankly, we find this machine boring. Also, the odds on hitting the big jackpot with 8 reels and 22 symbols per reel could be as high as 1 in 54,875,873,540 or one in almost 55 billion! We calculated the odds with only one queen per reel. The odds would be less if there are more than one queen per reel. Compared to the other dollar progressives with larger jackpots, it definitely does not offer the best opportunity to get rich. Slot players are paying a big "ransom" for these queens!

Nine-Line Giant

This variation of a video slot is really three 3-reel machines in one with three pay lines. Its attraction is that if there is no win on each play the coins bet are returned. It takes nine coins per handle pull. However, it plays left to right and right to left, with the traditional fruit symbols. So if you get a single cherry on only one line, you get two coins for nine. You seldom get your nine coins back. Also, it requires three cherries or three oranges in a row to get ten coins back. If you get nine cherries on the third payline, you win 1 million coins. For a quarter machine, that's $250,000. Payout for eight cherries is 25,000 coins and for seven cherries 2,500 coins.

A variation of the nine-line giant is the Totem Pole, which is a stack of three or more machines, requiring the multiple coins, but played with one handle pull. You may win on one, two, or even all of the machines each with its own individual paytable. This should be popular with players who like to play more than one or two machines, but we don't see much action on them. There are usually only one or two found in each casino.

CHAPTER 2

Percentages

All gaming machines, (slots, poker, keno, etc.) have been designed to pay back to the player a percentage of what is played. The amount varies with different types of machines and with different manufacturers. However, one thing is common among all machines, the payback percentage varies over time and will eventually approach the theoretical percentage.

If, for example, a particular machine is set to hold 4% from the player, that certainly doesn't mean that the player can expect to lose 4% of all the coins played over the first few hours, or even the first few days. For that short of time, virtually anything is possible. . . losing at a much greater rate, winning a little, winning a lot, or just breaking even.

The percentages for slot machines, and all other casino games for that matter, are based on long-term trials...tens of thousands, even hundreds of thousands of handle pulls, blackjack hands, or rolls of the dice. To really understand percentages, it's important that the player first understands the difference between short-term and long-term exposure. In the short term, percentages of 1%, 2% or even 3% against the player have little significance. But over the long term, those percentages become *very* significant and will tell you exactly what you can expect.

Slot players can boast of many short-term wins over the course of their life. In fact, it's always the short-term successes that most players remember. But unfortunately, those short-term sessions add up to long-term exposure. Few players win, then quit forever. That doesn't sound like much fun.

If you learn anything from this chapter, learn to limit your exposure... to "hit and run" as the seasoned players call it. No one has to tell you how easy it is to give all your winnings back.

Easy Calculations

The calculation of the payback percentage of a slot machine is a relatively straightforward procedure. It only gets complicated when you have a large number of winning combinations or a large number of reels. Originally, slot machines had 20 positions or stops on each reel. This means that on a three reel slot there are 20 x 20 x 20 = 8,000 different combinations of positions that the reels can stop on. That is called the "cycle."

In theory, if you play the machine 8,000 times, you should see every combination once. However, in reality you will see some combinations several times and some you might never see. If you played it 80,000 or 800,000 times you would probably see every combination. The longer you play the machine the closer the average results will be to the theoretical results.

What does this mean to you? Well, if there is one 7 on each reel, you would have 1 x 1 x 1 = 1 way of hitting three 7's in the 8,000 possible combinations. If there were four cherries on each reel, you would have 4 x 4 x 4 = 64 ways of hitting three cherries. Since there are more ways of hitting cherries than 7's, the cherries pay less than the 7's. The casinos and the manufacturers design these combinations of symbols called "reel strips" in order to ensure a desired payback.

The following drawings of symbols will help the reader understand the chart on page 33. The symbols are called "7-BAR," "5-BAR," and "1-BAR."

Since machines using these symbols typically have blank spaces also, many players refer to them as "ghost" machines. The term "ANY BAR" (AB) refers to any combination of bars on the payline, or in other words...no blanks.

Figure 1 is an actual reel strip calculation done by a manufacturer for one of its machines. the machine is a 2-coin, 3-reel machine with blanks and 1-BARs, 5-BARs and 7-BARs for symbols.

Section A shows how many of each symbol is on each reel. Section B indicates the payback percentage and the hit frequency. The hit frequency is the percentage of winning combinations to the cycle, i.e. $8,320/32,768 = 25.39\%$. That means that on average you will get a winner 25 out of every 100 times you play.

The second coin percentage is higher because of the bonus awards shown in section C. This is because three 5-BARs pays 50 coins if you play one coin and *150* coins if you play two coins. Three 7-BARs pays 200 coins on the first coin and *1000* coins on the second, as opposed to the normal doubling of the payout on the second coin. PLAYING THE MAXIMUM NUMBER OF COINS ON SLOT MACHINES ALMOST ALWAYS GETS THE BEST PAYBACK.

Section D shows the winning combinations and the calculations. Notice the 811 deductions listed on the ANY BAR (AB) pay line. This is a mathematical requirement as the 811 hits for the 1-BARs, 5-BARs and 7-BARs which pay more than the five coins for any three ANY BARs must be subtracted from the total ANY BAR hits. Finally, section E shows what percentage of the total payout each combination represents. As you can see, over 40% of the payouts are 5-coin ANY BAR pays.

figure 1

MODEL: 3-REEL 2-COIN ANY BAR WITH PAY ON BLANKS

32 STOP   CYCLE = 32768

A

SYMBOL	REEL1	REEL2	REEL3
1B	16	18	18
5B	9	9	9
7B	5	4	4
	2	1	1

B

COIN 1	PERCENT 86.97	HIT FREQ 25.39
	COINS 28,499	HITS 8,320
COIN 2	PERCENT 94.91	HIT FREQ 25.39
	COINS 62,198	HITS 8,320

C

BONUS AWARDS	
150	1000

D / **E**

COMBINATION					HITS	DEDUCT	PAYS	TOTALS COIN1	COIN2	PAYOUT %
—	—	16	18	18	5,184	0	1	5,184	10,368	18.2
AB	AB	16	14	14	3,136	811	5	11,625	23,250	40.8
1B	1B	9	9	9	729	0	10	7,290	14,580	25.6
5B	5B	5	4	4	80	0	50	4,000	12,000	14.0
7B	7B	2	1	1	2	0	200	400	2,000	1.4
								28,499	62,198	

"AB" MEANS "ANY BAR"

For progressive machines, there is no bonus on the maximum coin; you win the progressive jackpot instead. Our example of an 86.97% machine with a 5% progressive would result in a 91.97% machine overall. If this were a dollar machine, the progressive meter would start at $400 and would go up five cents for every dollar inserted. When you hit the big jackpot you get whatever is on the meter. The casino has been collecting 13.03% (86.97% payback) from the machine, and when it finally hits, they pay the amount on the meter and the overall casino percentage drops to 8.03% (91.97% payback). In the short term it might look like the machine paid too much, but in the long run the casino will make its percentage.

When mechanical and electro-mechanical machines were around, you could watch the reels spin and count the symbols in order to determine the percentage. Today, with most machines using microprocessors, there is no way of telling the percentage from the outside. In fact, unless you are the manufacturer, it would take thousands of dollars invested in "reverse engineering" to determine a machine's actual percentage. The machines use the reels as displays only, and in most cases they have nothing to do with how many times or in how many combinations the symbols will appear on the payline. When you consider that some of the machines can have as many as 256 computer-determined "stops" per reel, the odds of hitting the big jackpot could be *1 in 4 billion or more!*

With the old mechanical machines, each symbol on the reel represented a "stop," and there were generally 20 such stop positions as we've mentioned. So, to the average slot player facing a machine that looks like a good ol' mechanical but with a jackpot that looks too good to be true...it is!

The computer inside the slot machine has programmed those apparent 20 stops per reel to look like as many as 256! A clever deceit? Not really. Since the video-screen slot machines (you know, the ones with the "picture" of spinning reels) didn't go over so hot with the players, yet were the only way to offer really big jackpots, the casinos and manufacturers decided to restore the mechanical reel feature, but leave the computer inside! That's the microprocessor controlled mechanical. And that's what you see time and time again in the casino, especially where big jackpots are offered.

Don't think 20 x 20 x 20 for all the combinations... think 256 x 256 x 256 and get out your calculator.

When you use these extremely large numbers of stops on a machine, the large jackpot can become an insignificant part of the overall percentage, even if it is a million dollars or more. We joked with one casino owner about a possible 4 billion to 1 chance on hitting his giant machine if we put one 7 on each reel, and he said, "We'll give away the hotel and let the winner worry about the $ 5 million we're in debt."

I remarked, "It will probably hit the first day."

The owner countered, "If it does I'll be in Jamaica or the Bahamas, anywhere but here."

Figure 2 is an example of a more complicated reel strip. I'll leave this one to you to analyze if you are so inclined. Everyone enjoys a challenge.

figure 2

MODEL: 4-REEL 3-LINE TRIPLE BAR
25 STOP CYCLE = 390624

SYMBOL	REEL1	REEL2	REEL3	REEL4
CHerry	1	10	10	1
ORange	10	2	2	10
PLum	2	6	6	2
BEll	6	3	3	6
1Bar	3	1	2	3
2Bar	2	1	1	2
3Bar	1	2	1	1

COIN 1 PERCENT 92.058 HIT FREQ 10.689
COINS 359601 HITS 41756

COIN 5 PERCENT 92.740 HIT FREQ 32.069
COINS 1086806 HITS 125268

R1	R2	R3	R4	R1	R2	R3	R4	HITS	DEDUCT	PAYS	TOTALS
CH	—	—	—	1	15	25	24	9000	262	2	17476
—	—	—	CH	24	25	15	1	9000	262	2	17476
CH	CH	—	—	1	10	15	25	3750	0	5	18750
—	—	CH	CH	25	15	10	1	3750	0	5	18750
CH	CH	CH	—	1	10	10	24	2400	0	10	24000
—	CH	CH	CH	24	10	10	1	2400	0	10	24000
CH	CH	CH	CH	1	10	10	1	100	0	20	2000
OR	OR	—	—	10	2	2	15	600	0	10	6000
—	—	OR	OR	15	2	2	10	600	0	10	6000
OR	OR	OR	—	10	2	2	10	400	0	20	8000
PL	PL	—	—	2	6	6	23	1656	0	10	16560
—	—	PL	PL	23	6	6	2	1656	0	10	16560
PL	PL	PL	—	2	6	6	2	144	0	20	2880
BE	BE	—	—	6	3	3	19	1026	0	20	20520
—	—	BE	BE	19	3	3	6	1026	0	20	20520
BE	BE	BE	—	6	3	3	6	324	0	40	12960
1B	1B	—	—	3	2	22	1	132	0	60	7920
—	—	1B	1B	1	22	2	3	132	0	60	7920
1B	1B	1B	—	3	6	1	1	18	0	250	4500
2B	2B	—	—	1	2	23	1	46	0	100	4600
—	—	2B	2B	1	23	2	1	46	0	100	4600
2B	2B	2B	—	1	2	2	1	4	0	250	1000
3B	3B	—	—	2	24	1	1	48	0	200	9600
—	—	3B	3B	1	1	24	2	48	0	200	9600
AB	AB	—	—	24	24	1	1	576	96	20	9600
—	AB	AB	AB	24	2	2	19	1824	190	20	32680
CH	CH	CH	—	24	10	10	1	2400	0	10	24000
CH	—	—	CH	15	15	1	1	225	0	2	450
3B	3B	3B	3B	1	1	1	2	2	0	1000	2000

Figure 3 is an example of a 4-coin "Buy-Your-Pay" machine. This machine is one of the most frustrating ones in a casino. Each coin you enter enables or "buys" your payouts. So if you play one coin, only the cherries will pay. If you happen to line up the three BARs or the three $1,000 symbols and only have one or two coins in the machine, you won't get a thing.

I have seen many machines with three BARs lined up and only one coin had been played. No matter how much the player argues with the casino ("I know I put four coins in there!") he doesn't get paid.

This is probably the only type of machine where the more coins you play, the lower your percentage of return. If you don't play the maximum coins, however, your chances of missing a big payoff are greater. These machines do have reasonably high hit-frequencies but overall higher percentages, if you "buy" all "pays."

figure 3

MODEL: 4 COIN BUY YOUR PAY

25 STOPS   CYCLE 15625

COIN	%	HIT FREQ. %
1ST	95.4	33.8
2ND	92.2	39.8
3RD	93.5	40.8
4TH	92.5	40.9

R1	R2	R3
7	20	23
18	20	2
7	5	23
18	5	2
7	20	2
7	5	2

SYMBOL	REEL1	REEL2	REEL3
CHerry	7	5	2
ORange	5	4	5
BEll	5	5	6
MELon	1	1	1
BAR	5	3	10
$1000	2	7	1

PAYS	HITS	TOTAL
2	3220	6440
2	720	1440
5	805	4025
5	180	900
5	280	1400
10	70	700
	5275	14905

1ST COIN

CH	—	—	CH
—	CH	CH	CH
—	CH	—	CH
CH	CH	—	CH
CH	CH	CH	CH

2ND COIN			R1	R2	R3	HITS	PAYS	TOTAL
OR	OR	OR	5	4	5	100	10	1000
OR	OR	BAR	5	4	10	200	10	2000
BAR	BAR	OR	5	4	6	100	10	1000
BE	BE	BAR	5	5	6	150	18	2700
BE	BE	BE	5	5	10	250	18	4500
BAR	BE	BE	5	5	6	150	18	2700
MEL	MEL	MEL	1	1	1	1	20	20
						951		13920
						6226		28825

3RD COIN			R1	R2	R3	HITS	PAYS	TOTAL
BAR	BAR	BAR	5	3	10	150	100	15000
								43825

4TH COIN			R1	R2	R3	HITS	PAYS	TOTAL
1000	1000	1000	2	7	1	14	1000	14000
								57825

Poker Machine Percentages

Video poker machines are unlike slots in that you can see exactly what the percentage is for the machine and you can in turn shop around for the best machine to play. Figure 4 shows the most common pay tables and their corresponding payback percentages. All of these percentages have been determined empirically since there is no absolute method for calculating them. I have never seen a complete calculation for the theoretical percentage of a video draw poker machine. Although some pseudo-experts claim to have calculated it, I must revert to my Missouri born attitude of "show me" before I will believe it.

These percentages hold true for all denominations of machines with slight variations we call the "idiot factor." That is the degree of skill the player uses. A player's skill or lack thereof will result in an overall variance of only plus or minus 1%. (Unless we're dealing with actual walking, talking idiots.) Additionally, **the inclusion or exclusion of jacks or better in the pay schedule will result in an approximate 21% difference! Be careful!**

If you happen to find a machine with a slightly different pay table, you can estimate its percentages by whether its pays are a little higher or lower than the ones given in the table.

VIDEO POKER PAY TABLES

figure 4

						JOKERS WILD	DEUCES WILD
ROYAL FLUSH	250	250	250	250	250	400	250
FIVE OF A KIND WITH JOKERS						200	
FOUR DEUCES							200
ROYAL FLUSH WITH JOKERS						100	
ROYAL FLUSH WITH DEUCES							25
FIVE OF A KIND WITH DEUCES							15
STRAIGHT FLUSH	50	50	50	50	100	50	9
FOUR OF A KIND	25	25	25	25	50	15	5
FULL HOUSE	9	8	7	6	12	7	3
FLUSH	6	5	5	5	8	5	2
STRAIGHT	4	4	4	4	6	3	2
THREE OF A KIND	3	3	3	3	3	2	1
TWO PAIR	2	2	2	2	2	1	—
JACKS OR BETTER	1	1	1	1	0	*1	—
PERCENTAGES	96	93	92.5	92	88		

*Jokers Wild machines typically pay on Kings or better. Amounts shown are for 1 coin played. Percentages reflect all payouts including the typical 4,000 coin incentive award for maximum coins played. The 88% table is for nickel machines, of which there are not a great number available, even in Las Vegas. All other machines are quarters. Although the payouts for harder wins on the nickel machine are much higher than for the quarter machines, the absence of an even-money payout for Jacks or better more than makes up for the apparent "advantage" by costing the player 20%! The same can be said for the Deuces Wild machines whereby the absence of payouts for a high pair or two pair costs the player dearly and helps compensate for the apparent "advantage" of wild cards. All factors taken into account, it can be estimated that the Wild Card machines as listed here are in the 92 to 95% range.

The following chart is an example of how the casino relies on its computer system to keep an accurate record of all the slot machine activity and performance. The chart is generated weekly, monthly, and year-to-date.

TYPICAL CASINO'S SLOT MACHINE SUMMARY

MACHINE NO.	HANDLE	WIN	YIELD	THEOR YIELD
0101	13742.30	3153.65	22.9	17.0
0102	14154.85	3222.40	22.7	17.0
0105	31042.60	3466.00	11.2	9.3
0106	33680.30	3754.70	11.1	9.3
0108	21539.95	4095.65	19.0	18.8
0110	41890.25	5330.80	12.7	11.3
0111	28254.30	2864.35	10.1	10.0
0112	20696.40	2530.15	12.2	12.5*
0115	26025.85	3010.65	11.6	9.8
0116	10239.55	105.70-	1.0-	17.0*
0117	9908.65	2146.00	21.7	17.0
0118	18350.50	2860.85	15.6	12.5
0121	33858.40	3932.40	11.6	9.3
0122	16060.90	2449.30	15.3	17.0*
0124	14259.85	3102.85	21.8	17.0
0125	13350.10	2267.30	17.0	17.0
0126	12660.80	2579.40	20.4	17.0
0128	11261.45	2213.95	19.7	17.0
0129	18789.10	2298.50	12.2	12.2
0131	23677.90	2484.60	10.5	9.3
0132	33694.65	3947.85	11.7	9.3
0133	16012.65	2370.55	14.8	11.3
0135	19311.50	1860.35	9.6	9.8*
0136	12658.55	1714.40	13.5	10.0
0137	15635.65	2307.50	14.8	11.3
0138	11248.40	2369.65	21.1	18.8
0140	11355.00	1767.75	15.6	12.5
0142	9364.35	1284.85	13.7	11.3
0143	19638.05	2413.10	12.3	9.2
0146	9057.10	1728.95	19.1	18.8
0147	11595.35	2275.60	19.6	18.8
0148	12875.30	1941.65	15.1	12.5
0151	6546.70	1149.25	17.6	17.0
0152	9394.70	1913.25	20.4	18.8
0153	7279.95	1357.60	18.6	17.0
0155	12759.10	1966.80	15.4	12.5
0157	6731.20	1264.50	18.8	17.0
0158	5641.55	1112.25	19.7	17.0
0159	17342.30	2528.85	14.6	12.5
0160	22272.65	2782.65	12.5	11.3
TOTALS	683858.70	97715.15		

The "handle" is the total of all coins played in a machine. The "win" is the amount the casino held as profit (also called "hold"), and the "yield" is the casino's win expressed as a percentage of the handle.

On this particular report, the performance of certain machines is less than the expected "theoretical" percentage as noted by an asterisk. You can be assured the slot manager will check those machines carefully. You can also be assured the casino does not freely give these reports out to slot players!

CHAPTER 3

SPECIALTY MACHINES

True slot machines are those which have the typical spinning reels (whether actual or on a video screen), a coin slot, and a handle to pull or button to push. They require no skill to play. All other machines or games are referred to as "specialty machines." In this category you'll find video poker, keno, 21 or blackjack, horse racing, paddle push, craps, roulette, and even bingo. The most widely played of these specialty machines are video poker first and keno second.

Video Poker

Video poker has captured the imagination and the purses of game players in a few short years more than any other game of "solitaire" in the world. It is rapidly becoming the most popular gambling game of all, second only to bingo which is found in states other than Nevada and New Jersey.

Several types of poker slot machines had first been developed many years ago but were merely reel type machines with cards that were flipped to draw the poker hand or reels that bore the playing card symbols. Sometimes there were hold buttons with a chance for a second draw. But these machines were never very popular with slot players who preferred the fruit and bar symbol machines.

One of the first video games to be widely marketed was blackjack or 21. Several different manufacturers had versions out and they were getting very popular. When Logan Pease, Chief Engineer at Fortune Coin (now IGT), decided to put out a video draw poker machine, he met with great opposition. Casinos, manufacturers, and Gaming Board members didn't think it would fly. Probably because blackjack tables and players have traditionally outnumbered poker players in the casinos.

However, Pease was persistent and Fortune put the video poker version out first with quarter and dollar machines.

Twelve nickel machines were then placed near the front door of Sam's Town on an experimental basis. The results were astounding. They were being played around the clock with players standing in line to grab one when it was released.

Pease had the last laugh when video poker soon out-distanced 21. It is currently giving traditional slots a run for the money, while 21's popularity is quickly fading.

Based on the game of five-card draw poker, the game is simple to learn because the winning hands are described on the award glass above the video screen. Novice players who would never consider sitting in on a poker game to learn or play against the professional gamblers, found a new challenge that was more entertaining than just pulling the handle of a slot machine.

Avid players we interviewed confessed to being "hooked" on video poker to the point that they have spent and lost more money on it than they would ever have dreamed of dropping into the one-armed bandits. They admit to marathon sessions of 24 hours at a time, pushing those buttons and watching that screen as though hypnotized, waiting for someone to snap their fingers and wake them up. They survive on the questionable nutrition of free drinks and a sandwich or hot dog grabbed and brought back to the machine to eat while they continue playing. Friends, relatives, or teams of players will literally hold each other's machines while they take a "break" for a nature call. Or a player will place a cup or coat on the chair or in the tray along with his coins to signal that the machine is "taken" and ask a total stranger to "watch" it for him.

Video Poker's Appeal

What is so appealing about video poker that joins players in an unidentified, informal, and mysterious fraternity with members who seem to understand and trust each

other? Why was video poker such an overnight success?
Let's look at a few reasons.

First, note that we refer to video poker as a game, not
just another slot machine. There's the key. It's no acci-
dent that the state authorities refer to "gambling" as
"gaming." The implications are that gaming is "recreational" and "respectable." On the other hand "gambling"
is a "vice" and is well-known and documented in the court
records, in the history books, and in the literature of the
world. Since competitive games were first invented (when-
ever that may have been), man has used them for pleasure
and profit, and preferably both.

The word "game" suggests a respectable recreation requiring a certain degree of skill by the players. There's the
second key. Video poker requires a certain skill (not much,
but a smattering of intelligence). Any moron can push
those buttons at random and possibly hit a winning hand
or a royal flush. (Our 3-year old son/grandson was doing
just that on a machine at the shop before he even knew
what the different cards represented or what a winning
hand was. He had a tray full of coins that lasted longer
than the bankroll of the average "skillful" player.) By
contrast, there is absolutely no skill required to insert a
coin and pull the handle of a slot machine. That's not a
game, that's gambling, pure and simple. But the video
poker player is faced with five cards which can be held or
discarded (partially or wholly) to try for a winning hand.
He must use his knowledge of what the different possibilities or odds are for drawing the right cards and has a
variety of choices.

Satisfaction of winning from slots is not as great as winning at video poker. Having had some influence on the
outcome of each hand makes the player feel he has

"earned" his money. How often have you heard someone say that money "earned" is more welcome than a "hand out?" Even if he is dealt a royal flush on the first five cards, he will rationalize his role in the outcome. After all, he knew just which machine to play, didn't he? Or, after he's played a number of hands, he "set up" the machine to deal it out, didn't he?

That feeling of control is another reason. Man invented the machine, so he must be smarter than his creation. Right? He can outsmart that robot in a simple game of draw poker, can't he? Remember that we referred to video poker as a "game of solitaire." Since he is not pitted against another human being, he is "king," and "chance" can be reduced to a minor role in the results. He is not just equal to his opponent, he is superior.

In *Casino Games,* John Gollehon's book that covers each casino game in detail, the author sums up the reasons why players would rather go up against a "friendly" machine, instead of a table full of professional gamblers:

"It's a proven fact that a great many people like to play poker, but are intimidated by the casino's poker parlors. Some people do not wish to join in at a live game against players they don't know. The poker machine is just that ... a machine. No intimidation. No apprehension. No strangers. And of course, there are no "tells" to read, and no bluffs to worry about. It's poker, but at the player's own pace, in the player's own world."

Other reasons for video poker's rapid popularity can be attributed to its design. It was designed to be a compact machine, with the player *sitting* in a padded chair eye-to-eye with the video screen. He does not have to stand to pull a handle that may give him a sore arm after playing very long. There are buttons to push, not handles to pull. A departure from the one-arm bandit image. Most of the seats have foot rests, since not everyone is comfortable sitting in chairs of the same height. Also, the manufacturers are very clever; they know that if a player is sitting at a machine, he is not likely to move away as fast if it isn't paying at first. He will merely put in more money or shift to the next seat if it is available. He is less likely to walk away from a machine that he has "primed" with a lot of money.

Besides, you sit down to play a card game at the tables, why not at the machine. Most of the time sitting is more comfortable, but some machines have the round coin trays on the stands below, and you have to straddle that bucket as if you were milking a cow. Of course, that's a minor discomfort if you happen to be milking the machine of its coins.

Other chairs are bolted so close to the machines that you end up with painful creases in your knees from being jammed against the sharp edges of the formica base on which the machines are mounted. And, since casinos use some of the same bases designed for regular slots where players stand, the machines are so close together that you have to be a contortionist to get in and out of the chair. Heaven help you if you drop a coin on the floor. You bump your head on your neighbor's machine, spill your drink, or lose your glasses bending down to retrieve it.

We saw one lady with a handy plastic stick with an adhesive tip on one end who skillfully retrieved her dropped coins without bending over. It was designed to break down into two or three sections, like a fancy pool cue, and was easily carried in her purse. (Someone is sitting on a potential fortune with that invention!)

Realizing these inconveniences, manufacturers are now designing table-top and bar-top machines with padded consoles which are more roomy and comfortable. The giants like the Golden Nugget and Caesars are installing these for Video Poker, Video Keno and Video 21. These enhancements are also directed at pleasing the new "high rollers" to slot playing, who insist on their creature comforts.

The popularity of video poker is spreading to other states where some games of chance are permitted but not all forms of gambling allowed. In July 1985, Montana legalized video poker in licensed liquor establishments with a limit of five machines per location. The IGT Players Edge Machine is being installed with modifications. There is no coin hopper or payout. Instead the machines print out tickets for winnings that are redeemable for cash. Maximum jackpot allowed is $100. Minnesota and the Dakotas are considering similiar legislation because of Montana's successful operation.

The Video Poker Program

The Fortune Coin machine (refined and manufactured by IGT) is still the most popular machine although many versions of video poker by other manufacturers are seen and are making inroads into the sales picture. It was built with a video monitor rather than reels. Below the screen a row of buttons is used to play the game; there are no handles to pull. Under the coin slot, a deal button is pushed for play after inserting one to four coins. If a fifth coin is inserted, the deal is automatic.

Five cards from a standard 52-card deck appear on the screen. Under each card is a hold button so the player can choose which cards to keep before pushing the draw button to replace the cards not held and to obtain, if lucky, a winning hand. The payout for each winning hand is displayed on the award glass above the screen so that the player may determine in advance what to expect. If the second hand turns out to be a winner, the type of hand (two pair, straight, full house, flush, straight flush, etc.) and "winner" are displayed on the screen. As the machine pays, the coins are counted on a meter also displayed on the screen. If the hand is not a winner, "game over" and "insert coin" are displayed and the machine is ready for the next hand. A "cancel" button allows you to change your hold cards before drawing if you change your mind or accidentally push the wrong hold button.

Most machines follow this basic playing format but sometimes the deal, draw and cancel buttons are on the right of the screen rather than below. Some machines also have a "stand" button if you are dealt a winning hand on the first five cards. **Just remember to push either all hold buttons or the stand button before drawing, or you will erase your winning hand.** Some machines have "discard" buttons instead of "hold" buttons. In that case you discard what you want to throw away. If you do not discard specific cards, the machine may give you a whole new hand on the "draw" or it may just count your original five cards as a loser. *Be sure you know which type of machine you are playing and don't push those buttons until you understand what you are doing.*

What most people don't know about these machines is how the cards are dealt from a 52-card deck to prevent the same card showing up on the "draw" after having been discarded. On most machines, when the program "deals" the first five cards, it also selects five more cards which are placed in a position right behind the ones displayed. Think of it as five stacks of two cards each, the top one face up and the bottom one face down. It is not a stack of five cards or the balance of the deck waiting in the background to be dealt in sequence from the top to replace the cards discarded from left to right as would be the case in a table game.

If the first card from the left is discarded (or not held), the card replacing it on the draw will be the card already selected and waiting behind it. If the second card is retained, the card selected and waiting behind it will not be displayed on the draw, and so on. If the card to the extreme right, for instance, is the only one discarded, the card waiting immediately behind it is the one to be displayed, not the first card from an invisible stack of five cards waiting. After the draw and win or loss, as the case may be, the machine deals the next hand from the 52-card deck.

If you made the wrong choice on the draw and the next hand deals you the cards you would like to have had, don't get upset; *they would not have been the ones you would have received if you had drawn differently.* The process of random selection for the symbols shown on a poker screen is the same as for any other micro-processor controlled slot machine as described in the chapter on how machines work.

Some Unique Variations

Although the 5-card draw video poker machine is the most widely accepted game, you will find some other interesting machines that you might want to try. Intermark has its version of 5-card draw with a double-down feature. If you have a winning hand, you can double your win if you beat a specific variety of cards displayed on the screen. If you push the "double" button, you will be paid either double your winnings or nothing. Other manufacturers' machines have a "Hi-Lo" choice button to double your money. This is a version of "Red Dog." We have found that most of the double features are designed to increase the casino's wins and the player's losses. The Intermark machines also have a "talking" feature. The voice tells you what your highest hand is on the deal. For the novice, the voice may help him select his cards. For the veteran players, it is a patronizing nuisance. Consequently, there is another button to push which turns off the audio "helper."

Joker's Wild or Deuces Wild are now rather popular varieties of 5-card draw. IGT's "Jokers Wild" is becoming almost as widely played as the straight version. The appeal of this machine is the additional possibilities for winning. You can get five-of-a-kind with the joker which pays the second largest jackpot, even more than a royal flush with a joker. The giant jackpot is the royal flush without the joker and is usually higher than the jackpot for a machine without the joker wild-card feature. On the other hand, Deuces Wild machines pay considerably less for all winning combinations because there are four wild cards instead of one wild joker. The joker or wild cards can be counted as a replacement for any other card to make up the highest winning combination for each hand. See the comparison of pay tables and then look carefully at each machine you play to determine whether or not the smaller return is worth the increased chance for a winning hand.

The newest variation on the market is Bally's "Second Chance" video draw poker. If you have a losing hand, you get a second chance to make it a winner by pushing the second chance button. It deals you a sixth card face down. You place your bet of any number of coins from 1 to the maximum. Your card is then revealed. Now you make your best poker hand out of the six cards showing, win or lose.

For instance, if you have A, K, Q, J, of Spades and 3 of Diamonds for a losing hand, you can try one more time to get the 10 of Spades for the Royal Flush. On other hands you might have a chance for several different winning hands if you have good cards to draw to. If you have a small win on the first draw, you are paid. No second chance to improve your win, as is the case with some Wild Card variations. We predict that this machine will be a great success.

Machines with 7-card stud poker were found in some casinos when video poker became so widely accepted. However, they did not receive enough play to compare with the 5-card draw types. You seldom see more than one or two in a casino now. Perhaps the game was too complicated for the average novice poker player, and he didn't feel like losing a lot of money trying to learn it from a machine. The games also took longer than the 5-card variety and, consequently, did not produce as much revenue.

Many nickel poker machines also require ten coins to be played to win the largest bonus jackpot for a royal flush. You can play from 1 to 10 coins and receive an incrementally increased win respectively, but nine coins played will net only the multiple of winning coins shown for each coin, with the bonus for the 10th coin considerably higher.

Some manufacturers now display the payout table on the screen rather than on a separate glass above the screen, so that with each coin played, you can see just what the expected return will be.

Another variation allows an almost unlimited number of coins to play to win a jackpot up to a maximum of l0,000 coins per hand.

The most widely accepted variation or refinement is the "credit" feature which builds your winnings in a bank in the machine until you push a "cash-out" or "collect" button. You push a "play credit" button to play one or more coins, or "play max credit" button to play the maximum coins without having to insert coins for each hand. Most new machines are being built with this format. Advantages are that you don't get dirty hands from handling so many coins, you can play faster and make money for the casino faster (or yourself, if you're lucky), and there are less malfunctions and hopper jams for the floormen and mechanics to correct. Also, they are quieter. Players who still like to hear the coins clinking in the tray were suspicious of them at first, but the day will come when they will probably replace all the other types. **The disadvantage to credit play is that too many players never push the "cash-out" button. They simply play off their credit until the marker reads "0." It would appear that "credit" for the slot player is about as dangerous as credit for the table-game players. Remember, the credit shown on your credit meter is *your* money. Take it!**

A variation of progressive video poker features a bank of machines with three progressive jackpots: The largest for a Royal Flush, second largest for a straight flush and third for four-of-a-kind. It was introduced at the Sands, Las Vegas, in the spring of 1986. We've also seen this type at the El Cortez.

Although they are not "video" poker, there are two

machines we should mention.

One is the "Casino Royal" Flip card machine by Games of Nevada. It actually has five stacks of 52 cards that shuffle before your eyes and simulate the poker table with a green felt field between the machine's glass and the flip cards. The pay table appears on the award glass and is further amplified for multiple coin play on a small video screen beside the award glass. The machine is played just like the video versions and payouts are essentially the same. The problem with the flip card version is that each hand takes at least five times as long to play.

The other variation is "Reel" poker, a true slot machine with all the cards displayed on the five spinning reels. The odds on these machines would be calculated like any other slot machine, not like those on true poker machines.

The comparison of typical payouts for video poker both for regular and wild card types is shown in Figure 5.

The higher payouts for the maximum coins played is called the "incentive award." There are other variations depending upon the particular incentive that a casino may want to offer. For instance, some casinos offer an additional incentive of 4,700 or 4,780 coins for a Royal Flush on a straight poker machine as well as those with Jokers Wild. The incentive is for a jackpot of $1,175 or $1,195, just under the $1,200 that must be recorded and reported to the IRS. Some casinos also offer 20 coins returned instead of 15 for 4-of-a-kind on a Joker's Wild machine. Note also that progressive jackpots always have a smaller payout for the flushes and full houses.

The payouts may differ with the manufacturer, the casino, the location and the denomination. Nickel machines will pay 250 coins (12.50) on the 5th coin for 4-of-a-kind and 500 (25.00) coins for a straight flush.

figure 5

VIDEO POKER PAY TABLES

						JOKERS WILD	DEUCES WILD
ROYAL FLUSH	250	250	250	250	250	400	250
FIVE OF A KIND WITH JOKERS						200	
FOUR DEUCES							200
ROYAL FLUSH WITH JOKERS						100	
ROYAL FLUSH WITH DEUCES							25
FIVE OF A KIND WITH DEUCES							15
STRAIGHT FLUSH	50	50	50	50	100	50	9
FOUR OF A KIND	25	25	25	25	50	15	5
FULL HOUSE	9	8	7	6	12	7	3
FLUSH	6	5	5	5	8	5	2
STRAIGHT	4	4	4	4	6	3	2
THREE OF A KIND	3	3	3	3	3	2	1
TWO PAIR	2	2	2	2	2	1	—
JACKS OR BETTER	1	1	1	1	0	*1	—
PERCENTAGES	96	93	92.5	92	88		

*Jokers Wild machines typically pay on Kings or better. Amounts shown are for 1 coin played. Percentages reflect all payouts including the typical 4,000 coin incentive award for maximum coins played. The 88% table is for nickel machines, of which there are not a great number available, even in Las Vegas. All other machines are quarters. Although the payouts for harder wins on the nickel machine are much higher than for the quarter machines, the absence of an even-money payout for Jacks or better more than makes up for the apparent "advantage" by costing the player 20%! The same can be said for the Deuces Wild machines whereby the absence of payouts for a high pair or two pair costs the player dearly and helps compensate for the apparent "advantage" of wild cards. All factors taken into account, it can be estimated that the Wild Card machines as listed here are in the 92 to 95% range.

Most nickel machines do not return your bet on Jacks or better, although there are some that do. Also, many nickel machines require 10 coins played to win the highest jackpot.

Always study the award table on the machine you play to know what you can expect to win.

A man who regularly played video poker progressive machines at the Frontier Hotel hit two big jackpots within two months. Then, he walked in one night and found his favorite machines gone, replaced by a race and sports book. Two nights later he went back and found the machines and, you guessed it...he hit another one." *Three* royal flushes in two months!

Natalea Marshall, a grandmother from Calgary, Canada, complained of pains in her arms from playing slots. However, her Corvette, won on a quarter video poker machine at the California Hotel in Las Vegas, should help her forget the pain.

Everette Underwood, a pipeline operator hit a video poker machine at the Peppermill Casino, Reno, for $10,000 after investing $48 and playing thirty minutes. Two days later he sat at the same bar and hit another video poker machine for $10,000. He had plunked the first jackpot down on a truck and paid off the balance with the second. The $10,000 jackpots for a Royal Flush are on special IGT machines which also pay $25,000 for a "heart" royal flush in sequence (A,K,Q,J,10).

At the Tropicana, Joseph Kaled from California played a video poker progressive and hit a royal flush for $45,000. Less than four months later he hit another royal for a progressive jackpot of $41,319.30. Tropicana officials calculated the odds of drawing two progressive royal flushes in four months (based on his amount of play) as 70,000 to one.

Do you think that's an impressive coincidence? One month earlier, also at the Trop, June Kelp won $28,836 for a Royal Flush on a $5 video poker machine. The next day she got another Royal on the same machine for $20,000. The casino figured the odds of hitting two royal flushes on the same machine in two days (again, based on her play) as 80,000 to one. (The odds of hitting a royal flush are approximately 40,000 to 1, so you can see how they determined her odds.)*

On special quarter machines at the California Hotel in downtown Vegas, a "heart royal flush" in proper sequence is worth $25,000 or a new car, usually a Mercedes-Benz.

At Sam's Town in Las Vegas, on a special quarter machine a heart royal flush in any sequence wins an extra $2,500 besides the $1,000 regular payout. On special half-dollar machines at Sam's, a spade royal flush in any sequence will win a bonus of $5,000 for a nice total of $7,000.

The Las Vegas Hilton has two $5 video poker machines on trial manufactured by P & M of Las Vegas. Maximum jackpot is $20,000. Sam's Town also has $5 video poker with three coins maximum to win the Royal Flush for a $15,000 jackpot.

Video Poker Tournaments

The Royal Flush Club at Sam's Town in Las Vegas runs for a calendar year. Players register and receive a

*The casino's calculation seems much too low, unless the machine was played on a nearly continuous basis. The fact that it was hit on the same machine is incidental for the odds computation, since we can assume all other like machines had the same probability of winning.

numbered card. Each time they hit a royal flush on a video poker machine with the maximum coins played, a floorman registers the amount on a record card kept by the casino. With the first royal flush on any nickel, quarter, fifty-cent or dollar machine, the player receives a free Sam's Town jacket with a Royal Flush Club patch. The jackets sell for approximately $40. Quarterly bonuses are paid to the player with the most royal flushes in each of the four denominations ($500 for nickels, $1,000 for quarters, $2,000 for fifty-cents and $4,000 for dollars.) At the end of the year, additional bonuses were paid for the most royals hit during the year ($1,000, $2,000, $4,000 and $8,000 respectively). Their super special bonus was for the one member who hit the highest dollar amount in royal flushes for the year, a whopping $25,000! And all this is at no charge, no entry fee! It's the icing on top of the regular bonus jackpot for getting the royal flush with the maximum coins played. Sam's Town ran out of the first 1,000 jackets in about six weeks and had to reorder more. By far, this was the best promotion for the money! It was a "royal" promotion for sure!

The Frontier Hotel announced a weekly Monday night video poker tournament with a $40 entry fee in which you can win as much as $2000 for first place, $350 for second and $50 each for 3rd through 13th.

The top annual award given by "Gaming & Wagering Business" for the best slot promotion went to the Trump Casino Hotel, Atlantic City, for their "Are you in?" Poker Slot Tournament. Advertisements featured pictures of "Amarillo Slim" Preston and players got to compete with that real poker champion at the hotel's poker slot machines. Novice and so-so players could take a chance against a professional poker player when they wouldn't even think of attempting to face him at a real table game. At the slot machines, he's a "reel" opponent but not their "real" opponent which, of course, is the machine. Amarillo Slim is faced with the same odds on the machine as anyone else. His only advantage might be his expertise in holding the most logical cards to draw to, or perhaps, his nerve in throwing away the obvious cards to go for a long shot. That is, "knowing when to hold'em and knowing when to fold'em."

RANK OF POKER HANDS
(IN ASCENDING VALUE)

HAND	DESCRIPTION
Jacks-or-Better	Any pair of Jacks, Queens, Kings or Aces.
Two Pair	Two pairs of equal value cards such as two 3's and two 10's.
Three-of-a-Kind	Any three cards of the same value such as three Queens.
Straight	Any five cards in *consecutive* value, not of the same suit, such as 4 of clubs, 5 of hearts, 6 and 7 of spades, and 8 of diamonds.
Flush	Any five cards of the same suit, such as 8, 10, Jack, King, and ace of hearts.
Full House	Five cards that include a pair and three-of-a-kind, such as a pair of Kings and three 10's.
Four-of-a-Kind	Any four cards of the same value (all four cards of the four different suits) such as the 8 of hearts, diamonds, spades, and clubs.
Straight Flush	Any five cards in consecutive value, *of the same suit*, such as 2, 3, 4, 5, and 6 of diamonds.
Royal Flush	*Only* the 10, Jack, Queen, King, and ace *of the same suit*.

It should be noted that the differences in card value is of no consequence to the poker machine player (except single pair "jacks-or-better"). For example, three 2's pays the same as three aces. As a standard poker rule, the ace may count as either high or low in making a straight, A-2-3-4-5, or 10-J-Q-K-A.

Poker tournaments are not as prevalent as slot tournaments. Probably because they don't have to coax the poker players to keep the machines occupied. We suspect that the many slot tournaments may even be an attempt to keep true slots from being completely replaced by video poker. Even on the Las Vegas Strip, poker machines are being allotted more space than slots.

Keno

Next to regular slots and video poker, the third most popular machine is keno. Based on the live keno game, the most common version has a board of 80 numbers displayed on the screen from which you can choose from two to ten numbers per game, marked on the screen with a light pen (IGT's version) or selected by pushing the numbered buttons below the screen (American Coin Enterprises version). You then push a "start" button and 20 of the numbers are lit with your hits marked with an "X" or check mark. As in live Keno, if your numbers are selected, you win, provided you hit the minimum or more required as indicated on the award glass or the video screen. For example, you must hit four of eight numbers picked to get your money back, with the win increasing for more numbers hit. If you pick ten numbers and hit ten, you get the highest jackpot available, depending upon whether or not you are playing a standard payout or a progressive jackpot machine. You can play one to four coins with the maximum required to win the biggest jackpot. A typical award glass (pay table) follows:

	SPOTS MARKED								
SPOTS HIT	2	3	4	5	6	7	8	9	10
2	14	2	2	—	—	—	—	—	—
3		40	3	2	2	1	—	—	—
4			100	14	4	2	1	1	—
5				800	92	15	12	3	3
6					1,500	348	112	47	28
7						7,760	1,500	352	140
8							8,000	4,700	1,000
9								9,000	4,800
10									10,000

The table shows the amount won for one coin played. For more than one coin, multiply by the number of coins played to determine amount of expected win. On many machines, the jackpot for ten hits out of ten picks with four coins played is 50,000 coins instead of 40,000 or the progressive jackpot, an incentive feature to encourage you to play the maximum.

If you are not familiar with the game of keno, read all the instructions on the machine carefully. (And on all other types of machines, for that matter.) **Make sure you know whether the award table or the progressive jackpot amount is stated in coins or dollars; there are both types. For instance, "50,000" could mean 50 thousand dollars or 50,000 nickels, which is only $2,500! Fifty thousand quarters is only $12,500. Remember this rule no matter what type of machine you play, whether it be keno, video poker, slots or other specialty machines.**

Also, look for the progressive jackpot that offers the highest wins for your investment. Play smart. Some progressive jackpots for slots (not necessarily keno machines) actually start at an amount less than the usual incentive award for maximum coins on a non-progressive machine. Avoid them, please! The odds are high enough against you without giving the casino the extra advantage. Plenty of unwary players will soon build it up until it exceeds the incentive award.

For example, we were in a casino recently observing the keno progressives. Along one wall were two banks of nickel machines, separated only by a column. One progressive jackpot displayed $75,959. The other displayed $5,360. There were just as many players at each bank of eleven machines with several vacant seats in both. Obviously one had been hit recently. *Why would anyone play the same type of game and machine for five grand when he could be investing the same amount for 75 grand?* Of course, if you don't play the maximum coins, it doesn't matter.

Some slot players have also confessed that they never play for a jackpot over $1,200 because they don't want to fill out the IRS reporting form. But most players' intelligence is not even equal to their greed or their foolishness. Some players trying for the five grand were playing four coins each hand. Other players at the 75 grand bank were playing one coin at a time. We went away shaking our heads.

What are the odds of hitting a keno machine jackpot? It's all in the program. Only the manufacturer and the casino know for sure. The theoretical probability of hitting 10 numbers out of 10 should be about 9,000,000 to 1, same as in live keno, where the percentages against the player can exceed 25%! Be extremely careful if you decide to play either the live or electronic game.

Mini-Keno

This new type of keno machine manufactured by Games of Nevada displays only 40 numbers to pick from with a requirement of six hits for six numbers picked with four coins played to win the progressive jackpot. With one coin, six of six wins 1,600 coins. According to the feature glass, you can win 48,000 coins with the maximum coins played. We saw a bank of ten nickel machines linked to a progressive jackpot which on our visit was only $571. That's considerably less than 48,000 nickels or $2400. To win the

48,000 coin jackpot you have to match ten out of ten with maximum coins played.

Lots o' luck!

"21" Or Blackjack Machines

These video machines were developed before video poker and were quite popular when introduced, but are being "aced out" by video poker and even keno. Their decline in popularity is probably because of the limited win amounts compared to video poker, keno, and ordinary slot machines. There are no giant progressive jackpots to be won.

The game is essentially the same as the table game with a few extra incentives. Cards are dealt on the video screen in two sections, one for the player and one for the dealer, just as at the table. Rules of play are the same. If you get "21" or under and the dealer's cards add up to less than yours or he goes "bust" by going over 21, you win. After your first two cards are dealt, face up, you can choose to "stand" or take one or more additional "hits" by pressing the appropriate button. After you stand or "bust," the dealer's "hole" card is revealed as in most table games. The machine must hit on 16 and stand on 17. The theoretical odds on this game are the same as at the tables.

In most machines you can bet one to five coins, and if you win, you double your wager (pays even money). Always read all the instructions before you play so you know what to expect. Some differences from the table game and variations in machines to watch for are:

1. Unlike many table games, only one 52-card deck is used. It is "shuffled" by the computer program

sometimes after each hand and sometimes after 30 to 40 cards are dealt. In the latter case, there will be a pause while the machine "shuffles" and that notice will be shown on the screen. In either case, it is virtually impossible to "count cards" to increase your chances of winning. . . and hardly worth the effort.

2. On some machines, pushes (ties) will not return your bet. On other machines you may get your bet back.

3. Most older machines did not allow for double-down bets for 10 or 11 on the first two cards or multiple bets to splits pairs. These features have been added to some of the newer machines.

4. Some of the newer machines have also added insurance and surrender features.

5. Some new machines pay a bonus (1,250 coins) if you draw four aces on a winning hand. Other machines pay extra if you draw six cards and do not go over 21. Some machines pay double for blackjack.

6. Some machines will pay one and a half times your bet for "blackjack" with maximum coins bet.

7. The IGT version allows you to let your winnings "ride" on the next hand, up to a maximum of 400 coins.

The game is not as popular with players looking for instant wealth. For example, the maximum win for a single hand would be 800 coins or 1,600 coins with a double down on 400 coins bet. You won't get rich playing "21." Likewise, the casino's revenue from the machines is not as high as from regular slots, video poker or video keno. For players who want entertainment and who like the game, it can be played with only a few coins for "fun." Quite obviously, electronic blackjack machines are not for serious blackjack players. But for those of you who

might be intimidated by the live game, try the machines...
although there's really no reason in the world to feel un-
comfortable at a $2 blackjack table. The Blackjack
machines can be just as risky!

Horse Racing Machines

Like the sport of kings itself, the development of racing slots has an interesting history with a "colorful" cast
of characters.

One of the early attempts at developing and marketing
a horse racing slot machine was by a person with suspected
ties to groups "unacceptable" in the gaming industry.

A video tape racing machine was developed using actual races on cartridge tapes displayed on a video screen.
However, with questionable business practices reported,
the machine was never approved by the gaming authorities. Also the tape technology was not advanced enough
for the demands of a slot machine.

Later, a similar machine appeared under the name
"Video Turf," this time under the ownership of Gimbel
of Gimbel's department store fame. Mr. Gimbel was also
the one who financed the expedition to find the sunken
ship "Andrea Doria" and who had the safe recovered and
opened on television, in a pool of water with live sharks.
However, to our knowledge his machine never left the
post.

Other machines have been developed and can be found
in many casinos. Using the video disc, the RNG selects a
race and displays the actual horse or dog race on the screen.
Odds are displayed and eight horses or dogs are paraded
on the screen so that you can select your favorite from the

odds displayed and your "knowledge" after viewing the contenders. The machine's display of numbers to choose matches the "colors" or "silks" worn by the contenders in the race, i.e. blue, green, stripes, checks, etc. The race is run and winners paid.

The two most popular of the video disc types are a single player manufactured by P & M Coin and a two-player machine manufactured by Games of Nevada. You will find two or three of these machines in most casinos and hear players screaming at the screen as the horses round the final turn toward the finish line

The other type of horse racing machine that has become quite popular is "Sigma Derby" developed by Sigma, of course. It is a mechanical machine with five horses that run around a track. Ten or twelve players sit around the track and make their wagers based on the odds displayed for each race. Bets have to be on a Quinella, that is, the horses that finish in first and second position. Highest payout possible is 200 to 1 odds, i.e. 200 coins for each coin bet. Maximum number of coins possible bet is 99 per Quinella.

Sigma Derby is probably Sigma's most popular game. It is often found strategically placed either near the entrance to the casino or near the "live" race and sports book. Since it is a multiple player machine, it requires a license fee for each player position. The machines provide both off-hour action for the live race enthusiasts and rather inexpensive race-track action for players who like the Sport of Kings but have a peasant's purse. *Players who know little about interpreting racing forms or have little familiarity with the strategy of placing bets at the window find it an entertaining change of pace from the one-armed bandits.*

Although Sigma Derby is a mechanical race, the selection of the races and the control of odds and payouts is by microprocessors and the RNG. So you won't be able to memorize a sequence of races or predict the winner every time. As in all kinds of electronic casino games, the "derby" is no place for serious money.

Pusher Games

This machine goes by different names depending on the manufacturer. IGT's version is called "Whirl-Win." Another manufacturer calls it "Flip-It." It is based on an old arcade-type game which has two or three shelves on which coins lie and are pushed from one shelf to the other by mechanical paddles. Play is by inserting coins in one to four slots. An impeller shoots the inserted coin up on to the shelves or for an instant win into one of five holes or baskets on the wall above the shelves. These catchers are labeled $1, $2.50, $5.00, $10.00 or $25.00, the amount of instant win if your coin goes in. If your coin lands on a shelf, it may knock other coins down into the payout slot or land in a spot that allows the paddles to push other coins over the edge and into the payout slot.*

You're not apt to win a waterfall of coins on this game; a few dollars is the most you can hope for and a maximum of $25.00 per coin played if you scored the highest each time.

Try a few coins in this one for luck. But if you have big bucks in mind, paddle your canoe on by them.

---

*The coins at the edge are precariously close to falling into the payout slot, and the greedy urge to "bump" the machine (just a little) has tempted us all.

Hold and Draw Bingo

Sometimes called "Bingo Poker" these new machines have been tested in a few casinos, but over the past year none have stayed very long. As the name suggests, it combines the features of both video poker and bingo. Bingo cards are displayed on the screen with a group of numbers "called" and marked. You may choose to hold those numbers that you think will line up for a row of five to "Bingo" and draw replacement numbers for those discarded, as in Poker. Five numbers in a row, horizontally, vertically or diagonally will win. The combination of the two games just doesn't seem to hold the player's interest. At least, it didn't keep us entertained very long.

Bingo Machines

Several types of bingo machines have been developed, and casinos place a few of them near the entrance and exits to bingo parlors for between session play by bingo fans.

Some of these machines display only one board with the "called" numbers appearing after a handle pull or pressed button. Others display four to eight boards for a chance to win more than one bingo per game. Options include playing the same board for several games (as in keno machines) or by changing boards each hand or as often as you wish.

We haven't seen many of them and they don't seem to last long on the casino floor either.

Numbers Game

Sigma Game, Inc. placed their "Lucky Numbers" machine in six Las Vegas casinos: Circus Circus, Slots-O-Fun, Palace Station, Gold Coast, Silver Nugget and Golden Nugget. The player can activate one to five reels per play. Each reel contains the figures 0 to 9 twice plus one joker which is wild. A play of one reel only can win seven coins for hitting the number or a joker. Maximum jackpot is 10,000 coins. The 7-1 odds result from three chances to hit a single number out of 23 reel positions.

Games of Nevada has a numbers game out with two different pay tables. If you match particular colors also, you win even more.

These machines may become popular with avid lottery players or with players who are very superstitious about numbers.

Video Craps

Many different versions of dice games have been tried in the slot arena but most have "crapped out." One of the reasons may be that the rules and multiple ways of wagering are too complicated for the average slot player. Maybe it's because crap shooters prefer "live" action and there is no substitute for the excitement of cashing in on a hot shooter's roll.

Status Game Corporation placed its video crap game on field trial at Caesars Palace recently. The game features two screens, one which shows actors playing the game. The other shows the craps layout. When a player pushes the "roll" button the computer-generated dice roll shows on screen as if it had been rolled by the actors. Players can bet up to 40 quarters. Rules of the game are printed on the console and could actually teach people how to play craps without the intimidation of a live game.

Video Roulette

There's also a similar game for roulette, using an actual wheel protected inside a clear plastic bubble, an electronic table for placing bets, but no dealers. The machine tells you to "place your bets," tells you if you won, and tells you if you lost. It's a wonder it doesn't tell you when to go to the bathroom.

A casino executive told me recently that he's afraid someday the entire casino will be nothing but buttons to push and machines that talk. No dealers, no pit bosses, just buttons and weird voices.

Let's hope not.

CHAPTER 4

Jackpots

Beginner's Luck

On his *first* trip to Las Vegas, Joe Moroski of Ashtebula hit a Lady Luck progressive quarter machine for $45,000.

James Kornapes of Texas lined up three wild jokers on a $25 slot machine at the Flamingo Hilton and won $25,000. It was his *first* trip to Las Vegas.

Steven Spieldenner, 22, from Ohio went home rich after his *first* trip to Las Vegas. He was attending a convention and had just seen a show in Bally's Celebrity Room. Coming out afterwards, he stopped at a progressive quarter slot and after putting in only $10.00 (only $10.00?) hit four 7's for a nice $47,258!

John Goodman, a business finance major at Phoenix Community College dreamed of becoming a millionaire by the time he reached age 35. At age 23, he made a "spur of the moment" trip to Las Vegas with a friend to gamble for about five hours. The two were playing side by side on the 19-machine Maximus Millions slot carousel at Caesars Palace. He heard bells ring but didn't notice the five 7's lined up on the third coin pay line. He had never played a slot machine before. (He never played a slot machine before?) John put more money in and pulled the handle again but nothing happened. (ALWAYS CHECK ALL PAY LINES BEFORE AND AFTER YOU PULL THE HANDLE. IF YOUR MACHINE DOES NOT LOCK UP AND YOU PULL THE HANDLE BEFORE YOUR JACKPOT CAN BE VERIFIED AND PAID, YOU LOSE.) "I thought it was broken," he said. His friend leaned over, pointed to the five 7's and told him he had won. The jackpot was $1,077,777. Goodman had played the machine for two or three hours, investing $150 before he won.

Wearing blue jeans, tennis shoes and a slightly wrinkled tee shirt, Goodman had borrowed $100 from his friend because he had no money of his own to gamble with. Together with the minor payouts, most of the cash was almost gone, and he was reluctantly considering whether or not to negotiate another loan from his friend when he scored.

Later, Caesars officials treated Goodman and his friend to a dinner of barbeque ribs, shrimp and Dom Perignon champagne. Major Garrett, of the Las Vegas Review-Journal, reported Goodman as saying, "I remember it but couldn't taste anything. If it had all been wood, I wouldn't have noticed.''

Incidentally, the machine Goodman was playing was number 5114. The address where Goodman worked as a bookkeeper was 5114 N. 27th Ave. Add the digits in 5114. Elevens seem to go with sevens in the gambling industry. The jackpot was set to end in five sevens, to match the symbols that were necessary to hit it. Goodman didn't even notice the number of the machine he was playing, so it wasn't a matter of superstition in his case. He may become superstitious though after that coincidence. When he got back home, his friends probably called him ''John Goodrich.''

Goodman's win was the third $1 million plus jackpot at Caesars, Las Vegas. The first was for $1,065,358. The second was a record $2,599,552 hit by a Detroit housewife. She jumped up and down and hugged the machine. She had visited Caesars often with her husband, an automobile broker, and she always played the progressive dollar machines near the hotel entrance. On the day she hit the big one, she had invested less than $20.00. (Less than $20.00?) When she arrived for the awards ceremony the next day, she was wearing her new black mink coat, bought with part of her winnings.

Lorraine Page of California had been playing for several hours but only about three minutes on the "Million Dollar Baby" machine at Caesars Palace before lining up the four triple bars for a progressive jackpot of $1,150,697. (Only three minutes?) She kept running out of coins and had to dip into her husband's tray for the three lucky coins that made her Caesars' fourth million-dollar-winner.

Caesars' "Million Dollar Baby" may be a problem child for the casino. It was hit by a newlywed woman just two months after it was "born," and it had not yet accumulated the million dollar "jackpot reserve." It had finally recovered from the first payout only to be hit again three years later for $2.59 million. Then five months later for $1.15 million. Is Caesars ahead or behind?

All four of these million dollar plus jackpots paid by Caesars were paid at once, in one lump sum, unlike the lotteries and some other progressive jackpots that are paid in installments by annuities.

More Winners

John Raney from Maryland was playing a million dollar progressive at the Golden Nugget in Atlantic City. The machine broke down and he asked a friend to "hold" it for him until it was fixed, while he played another machine. He hit the million on the "relief" machine. He has plenty to put away for a "Rainy Day."

Ann Drew of California played $9.00 at Harrah's Reno and "drew" a $73,000 jackpot.

Harold Sorkazian a native of Syria who lives in California, arrived at the Las Vegas Hilton to enter their slot tournament. Before checking into his room he decided to play awhile. He lost $26 in ten minutes but lined up four 7's to win $2,138,350. He had previously won $250,000 almost two years to the day but said he lost it all back in the slots over an eleven-month period.

Three race horse symbols lined up on a progressive dollar machine for a $93,463 jackpot for Frieda Schusteritsch of New York after playing seven or eight minutes at the Frontier, Las Vegas. (Seven or eight minutes?) She was playing one machine with only an occasional pull on the machine next to it, trying to kill about two hours before her plane left. About the sixth occasional pull made her day.

A Michigan grandmother, Norma Harrison, played only six quarters at the Imperial Palace Hotel and Casino and went home with $33,442. (Only six quarters?) She visits Las Vegas annually. Now she can afford first class!

Richard and Micki McKinnon played a quarter progressive at Bally's Reno. Starting with only a handful of quarters, they filled their pockets with $159,405 and the keys to a Porsche 944 besides. (Spare me!)

Wayne Grimsley from California was anything but "grim" after winning $100,000 cash on a machine at Circus Circus, Las Vegas. Bet he "grinned" all the way to the bank.

Margie Johnson of New Jersey is a triple winner in two years at Harrah's Marina in Atlantic City. She hit $616,866. Later, she won $155,629 and a month later won $108,381. Margie was quoted in Lottery Player Magazine, "I'm not a degenerate gambler. It relaxes me. When I go to a casino, I don't think about my troubles. Some people go to psychiatrists. Some people take drugs. I go to the slots." (No wonder!)

A San Francisco school teacher who chose to remain anonymous hit a world's record jackpot of $3,041,864.40 at Harrah's Hotel-Casino in Stateline (Lake Tahoe), Nevada. "It's a fantasy, a dream. I came up here a hundredaire and I'm going home a millionaire." (How cute!)

Harriet Peterson, from New Jersey, invested $20 and won $200,000 at the Sands Atlantic City on the 4th of July, a nice day to become financially independent.

At Trump Plaza Atlantic City, Julio Fiorillo, a New Jersey bookkeeper, was waiting to be paid a small jackpot by an attendant and decided to play another machine. She hit $487,034 on the second machine.

A court reporter from California found her favorite machine at the Flamingo Hilton being played by someone else. So she played the machine next to it, slowly, hoping the other player would leave. She played $40.00 and lined up five sevens for the $250,000 Pot O'Gold.

Virginia Myers of Los Angeles hit a dollar machine at the Mint for $82,000 after playing only a few minutes. (Not again!)

Gregory Tavares hit a $140,000 jackpot at Harrah's Tahoe. Four months later he hit a dollar slot for $102,604, also at Harrah's.

At the Reno Hilton, Gerry Jones from California played the rainbow carousel and hit $250,000. Also, at the Reno Hilton, Eleanor Logsdon hit the $195,000 and qualified for their annual Championship Pot O'Gold Slot Tournament.

At the Claridge in Atlantic City, a young grandmother, who was ready to go home, stopped long enough to play $7.00 worth of quarters (Oh no!) and won a progressive jackpot of $161,778.00. She didn't get home that night because the hotel management treated her and her friends to deluxe overnight accommodations.

Rocco Dinubilo, a California raisin grower, hit a record jackpot of $2.47 million at Harrah's Tahoe. He had been playing blackjack earlier, but started playing the $1 progressive at about 2:00 a.m. At about 4:30 a.m. he hit $250 and a few minutes later lined up four triple bars for the big one. Gaming Control Board agents spent more than five hours examining the machine before pronouncing the jackpot legitimate. They were extremely cautious because the machine was on the same carousel as the $1.7 million *rigged* jackpot hit a few months before.

Rocco said he expected the close scrutiny by the gaming officials but knew they would find nothing wrong because he knows nothing about the machine's mechanics. "All I know is you pull the handle." Dinubilo told reporters he had read about the jackpot at home and told his friends he was "going to go get it." Queried as to how he felt about the big bite the IRS would take, he replied, "I'd be satisified with half of it."

Phillip Reszutek invested only $5.00 before winning $127,000 on a quarter progressive at the Hacienda. Taking a four-day respite from the cold climate of Minnesota, the Reszuteks were down about $500 before lining up the five seven's on the third line. They decided to take home new pairs of jeans to their two teenage sons instead of just tee shirts as originally planned. (Our guess is the kids would rather have some of the cash!)

Paul Maxwell of Utah attended a hunting show in Las Vegas and afterwards hit the Las Vegas Hilton's "Pot O'Gold" progressive for $250,000. He had played only $3.00.

Scott Milburn of Nevada, an electronic technician, hit a slot jackpot of $921,686 and "his and hers" Dodge automobiles at the former MGM Grand in Reno. He had invested $12,000 over an eight-month period. The day he won he had played $600 into a progressive dollar machine in the "Stairway to the Stars" carousel.

Milt and Sheila Fawcett and family from Canada were on their way to Disneyland when their mobile home broke down. While waiting for repairs, they played the slots at the Desert Inn in Las Vegas and hit a jackpot for $35,000.

Pat Mason of Florida won more than a million dollars on a three-reel dollar progressive at the Frontier Casino in Las Vegas. She will receive $50,000 per year for 20 years.

A group of players from Pennsylvania pooled their money for a recent gambling trip, each contributing $20 to the bankroll. Several of them played together at the Tropicana in Atlantic City and hit $341,241 in jackpots! Each received approximately $20,000 for his $20 investment. That's a hundred to one return. Not bad!

Let us give you a word of warning though. IF YOU ENTER SUCH A POOL WITH YOUR FRIENDS OR OTHERS, GET A CONTRACT IN WRITING AS TO HOW THE PROCEEDS ARE TO BE DIVIDED. Consider this: A young girl and a friend were playing three slot machines together at Harrah's Marina in Atlantic City. The girl's boyfriend and another fellow joined them, and all four were playing with the accumulated winnings. The girl left for a few minutes to arrange a breakfast for the group. She heard a commotion at the machines and learned that a member of her "team" had hit the $327,296 jackpot.

The lucky player refused to split the money. The girl sued. Eventually, a court ruled that the pooling of money "demonstrated an intent to make the winnings available to each other with the result that neither party could properly take possession of the funds to the exclusion of the other." A three judge panel in the Appellate Division of the Superior Court upheld the decision of the lower court and granted part of the jackpot to the young lady. SO, DON'T PUT YOURSELF THROUGH A LAWSUIT. GET AN AGREEMENT UP FRONT IN WRITING!

The first Pot-O-Gold winner at the Flamingo last year was Callie Mae Jingles, 66, of California. She won $250,000.00 after playing only five minutes. With a name like "Jingles," how could she lose. Callie said she would buy a house so her twelve grandchildren would "have a yard to play in" when they visit.

The second Pot-O-Gold winner at the Flamingo was Isabel Beyer of Minnesota who went to Las Vegas to celebrate her birthday. She received a nice present of $147,098.50. She played the machine for about one hour (what took her so long?) and invested approximately $65.00.

The third Flamingo winner of a Pot-O-Gold jackpot was Verla Fletcher of New York with a tidy $139,956.70. In the ten years she and her husband had been visiting Vegas, Verla had never played progressive machines before but decided to do so after dreaming she had won a progressive jackpot. She had been playing only about 20 minutes when her dream came true.

On Mother's Day, Sara Gilliam and her mother Mary from Kentucky were playing the Pot-O-Gold slots at the Flamingo. But it was the daughter who hit the $250,000 jackpot and was the fourth winner on that special bank of machines.

Anthony Lattanzio, 68, hit a record jackpot of $925,000 on a quarter machine at the Claridge Casino-Hotel in Atlantic City. Shortly afterward, he received ten marriage proposals from patrons and employees of the hotel. A week earlier he had played the same machine and lost $150. On this trip his friends had warned him not to play the same machine again. Luckily he didn't listen.

Geraldine Hendrickson of Illinois, hit the million dollar progressive at Caesars in Atlantic City after losing $200 of her $240 stake. When she realized she had hit the jackpot she screamed, "I love Caesars! I love Caesars!" She was the third million dollar winner in two years.

An 80-year-old grandmother decided she would rather

play slots than accompany her daughter and granddaughter to the beach. She won $400,000 at the New Jersey's Atlantis Casino Hotel.

The first million dollar slot machine jackpot in the world was hit by George Epp of Pleasantville, New Jersey, when he won $1,250,000 at the Golden Nugget in Atlantic City. With a win like that, anywhere he lived could be "Pleasantville."

Sheri Golfeder won $11,346 on a quarter progressive at Caesars Palace after only playing ten minutes. That's over $1100 per minute.

Pamela Cobb of Ohio was a double winner at the Holiday Casino on the Center Strip. She first won $500 on a quarter slot machine. A few days later after urging from her mother, she returned to the same machine and hit $16,000. (Always listen to your mother.)

At the Imperial Palace, Margaret Landas from California hit a nickel slot for $22,816.90. She planned to buy a car for her son. That's a healthy jackpot for a nickel machine.

At Sam's Town, Josephine Guidray from New Orleans won $9,905 on a dollar slot machine. She said she would share her winnings with her ten grandchildren and five great-grandchildren.

The record for the highest return for the smallest investment on a slot must be given to LeRoy Pfeiffer of Las Vegas. Pfeiffer invested only three nickels for one pull on a Sam's Town "Win A Million" nickel slot. He won $50,000 (one million nickels.)

A few years ago, the Las Vegas Hilton installed four $25 slot machines, each with a maximum jackpot of $15,000. The $25 tokens weigh one ounce and are pure silver. According to casino executives, in the first 30 hours of operation they paid out almost $250,000. That's the equivalent of one major jackpot every one and three-quarter hours. According to Jeff Payne, Slot Manager, the Hilton now has nine in operation. They are single line, three coin multipliers requiring $75 per pull to win the maximum jackpot of $15,000.

Back in 1984, the only Las Vegas hotels featuring slot machines with million dollar or more jackpots were the Barbary Coast, Caesars Palace, Riviera and Vegas World on the Strip. In Glitter Gulch the hotels that offered million dollar plus jackpots were the Fremont, Golden Nugget, Lady Luck and Las Vegas Club.

Today, million dollar jackpots are common at most all of the giant hotel-casinos.

Sally Gamache of Minnesota played a three-coin half-dollar machine at Circus Circus, Las Vegas. After a $40 investment, she took home a $92,000 Rolls Royce sedan.

Jerry Oland of Indiana drove home a red Corvette from the Stardust Hotel. He invested $5.25 in a quarter slot machine while waiting for his wife to finish packing to go home and won within five minutes.

Thomas Alalmo from California dropped 3 coins in a Circus Circus slot and won a $75,000 Ferrari.

Yoshihiro Uetake of Honolulu invested $30 in a slot machine at the California Hotel and won a Cadillac Seville.

Mary Etta Postier of California won a flame-red Ferrari after putting only nine quarters in a slot machine at Circus Circus. That's $2.25 and three pulls of the handle for a car that is worth approximately $60,000.

Fred and Viola Smurtz of Oxtail, Montana played the $1,000,000 Super Jackpot machines at Bally's starting the minute they arrived on a Friday night. By Tuesday of the next week, Fred and Viola had amassed a big $1,523 loss! But on Wednesday their luck changed, and they only lost another two hundred dollars between them. They went home losers.

What's the matter with these two clods? Everyone else in this chapter were big winners! Actually, we just wanted to see if you're still paying attention. Hearing about all these big winners can get downright boring, but we have a point to make.

We could fill this entire book with winner upon winner. We could fill ten times, maybe 50 times the pages in this book with big winners and more big winners. And we could fill the New York City Telephone Directory with the names of loser upon loser. Add the Los Angeles Area Telephone Directory, the Cleveland Telephone Directory ...well, you get the picture.

There are so few winners in comparison to losers, but it always looks like a lot of winners because there are so many players. And it's always the winners who get the publicity. Fred and Viola are the only exceptions.

CHAPTER 5

Common Misconceptions

Is winning at slot machines purely a matter of luck? The answer is unequivocally "yes." But many slot players insist that they know how to beat the machines. You've probably heard dozens of theories from slot players that they consider to be "sure fire" ways to win. Or, perhaps, other books on slot playing have included rules that sound good and may have worked at one time or at one place or another. Maybe you have formulated your own system of play. Let's examine a few of the most common theories we have heard repeatedly from players and try to determine if they have any merit.

MISCONCEPTION #1:
Play the machine nearest the door or on the aisle.

The reasoning behind this false idea is that casinos place higher payback percentage machines at high-traffic locations to give the impression that all the machines in the house have high payout percentages, which are commonly called "loose" slots. At one time this "bait and switch" routine may have been a common method of attracting the passing tourist. However, due to the current slot craze many casinos now enjoy the ideal situation—more players than machines. Many establishments have placed signs on the machines limiting one to a customer when other players are waiting, especially with video poker machines.

If there is any good reason to place the higher percentage machines on the aisles, we might wildly speculate that it's to give a slight edge to handicapped players in wheel chairs or those who must carry oxygen tanks and who have difficulty playing the "inside" machines that are so close together. However, we are probably giving the casinos more credit for compassion and generosity than they deserve. Realistically, the best reason to play the "end" machine is for your own comfort, i.e. you're not crowded by players on both sides. If these slots frequently pay more, it's probably because many people believe this theory and, consequently, the machines receive more play, thereby increasing the likelihood of the machine going through a "pay cycle." *Players think casinos are willing to lose on a few machines and make it up on the non-paying "sucker" machines. Not true! If any machine fails to hold its required percentage for the casino, it will be taken out of play or undergo a major inspection and overhaul by their mechanics or the manufacturer.*

MISCONCEPTION #2:
"Cold" Coins or "Fresh" Coins versus "Hot" Coins or "Used" Coins.

"I always play only with coins I have purchased; I never play the coins that come from the machine."

"Fresh coins, cold from the roll, will fool the machine into paying. Hot coins tell the machine it has already paid me, so it's time to clam up."

"If the coins coming out of the machine are cold, leave it. It's a cold machine."

"If the coins the machine pays are hot, play it, it's a hot machine."

"I touch the glass on the front of the machine. If it's hot, I play it; if it's cold, I don't."

These remarks or variations meaning the same thing were frequently heard from players interviewed. None are valid theories. Neither hot nor cold coins have any influence on the machine. The only possible difference the temperature of the coins could make is in the ease with which they move through the coin acceptor. Even then the minute difference due to cold contraction or heat expansion has no bearing on the operation of the machine. If coins get jammed in the acceptor, it's usually because the coins are nicked, bent or smashed out of shape, or there is damage to the acceptor itself. Such damage often occurs from players pushing other objects such as nail files or knife blades down the slot to release jammed coins.

The only reason coins come out of some machines hotter than from others is due to the proximity of the coin "hopper" to the electric lights or other electrical components in the machine and the length of time they have been sitting in the hopper near these heat producers. Some machines have hoppers closer to the lights or other heat generating components, some machines have more lights or higher wattage bulbs, or incandescent bulbs instead of fluorescent bulbs. For instance, a machine with the new stepper motor driving the reels will have more heat generated within the cabinet than one with the non-stepper motor. Also, a machine's cold glass is due to the number and type of light bulbs near the glass. There is absolutely no such thing as a literally "hot" or "cold" machine influencing the amount of payout. There could be a psychological influence on the player's attitude. Perhaps you don't like the feel of the hot coins. In that case, leave them in the tray awhile and they'll cool off or better yet, cash them in as advised in our section on money management.

MISCONCEPTION #3:
"I've put so much money in it, it has to be ready to hit."
We've heard this statement so many times that if numbers counted we'd begin to believe it. The truth is that there is no certainty that putting large amounts of money into a machine will make it pay. The random factor built into the programs is designed to eliminate any guarantee of a machine paying or not paying after a certain number of plays. Even though in the long term of weeks and months the percentage factor will average out, the pay cycle may not come around daily or weekly or at any other predictable time.

Further, there is no guaranteed length of a pay cycle which will include the large jackpot. *A given machine may pay out small amounts frequently and not hit the big one for months or even years. It's possible to do so and still hold its percentage.* Another machine may pay large amounts consistently for several hours or even days and the casino may have to refill the hopper several times before it goes into its non-pay cycle often referred to as a "cold streak." We use the word "cycle" loosely here since there is really no guarantee of a machine having any actual "cycle" or pattern of play or pay. See the section on how machines work for further explanation of "cycles."

You've heard the old saying, "Being in the right place at the right time." That's about what trying to predict when a machine is ready to hit boils down to.

MISCONCEPTION #4:
Watch for someone who has put a lot of money in a machine without winning. Play it; it should be ready to hit.

This theory is just a variation of the previous one and the explanation of its validity is the same. Again, let us emphasize: *The length of time or the amount of money played in a machine without its paying has no bearing on its readiness to pay.* It makes no difference whether you or someone else is playing. The machine is no respecter of persons. It doesn't know a lucky player from an unlucky one. It doesn't "care" or "know" how much you have played or paid. The machine is . . . after all, just a machine. Although the meters in the machine record the coins in and coins out, these meters have no influence on the random number generator that determines when the winning combinations are going to be displayed. Every time you're tempted to follow such bad advice, turn to the chapter on odds and percentages and how the machines work and re-read it.

MISCONCEPTION #5:
Casinos tighten or loosen the slots by flipping a switch or tightening a screw.

This common complaint by players is often related with

the "time" of play. Some players believe they tighten the machines in the day time and loosen them at night, or vice versa. Or they change them on weekends or holidays or during tourist season.

The technology exists to remotely control machines and to change percentages by "flipping a switch," to use the common terminology. However, the Gaming Control Board prohibits the use of such technology.

Although casinos may have their own personnel with the capability to change the payout percentage, it would not be economical for them to change the percentage daily, or even weekly or monthly. When hundreds of machines are on the floor, only a few could be changed at one time. According to John Stroup of the Flamingo Hilton, casinos obtain a manufacturer's license so that they are permitted to change the percentages, but they usually do not do so themselves. It's more cost effective to decide what their requirements are and let the manufacturer make the changes.

Most machines contain only one percentage program. A "chip" providing multiple percentages which can be changed by literally "turning it" is available, but the Gaming Control Board does not authorize its use. Changing the percentage in the microprocessor controlled machine is usually a matter of substituting a computer chip and changing the pay table on the glass. The new computer chip would change the number of coins paid for the given symbols on a video poker machine and the theoretical number of "reel" stops on a video slot machine. For instance, the IGT video poker Jokers Wild machine originally paid 20 coins for each coin played for a line-up of four-of-a-kind. Now, at most casinos, the payout has been reduced from 20 to 15 for four-of-a-kind, but all other payouts remain the same.

MISCONCEPTION #6:
If a machine is not paying, don't play the maximum number of coins. Drop down and then increase to the maximum when it starts to pay.

The idea behind this theory is that you'll save money "priming" the machine for the big jackpot. Again, the number of coins played has absolutely no effect on determining when or what type of winning symbols will appear on the machine.

One mathematical "genius" was sure he had a system of play that would assure a greater return for fewer coins played. His system was based on the Fibonacci sequence (1, 2, 3, 5, 8, 13, 21, etc.) For you non-mathematicians, Leonardo of Pisa, or Leonardo Fibonacci, the greatest European mathematician before the Renaissance, originated the sequence in 1202 as an exercise in addition. As you can see, each number in the sequence is the sum of the previous two numbers. This slot player determined the number of coins to play based on that sequence.

For instance, on the first, second and third pulls he would play the maximum number since each of the combinations in the sequence was supposed to be a winner. On the fourth pull he would only play one coin. On the fifth pull, the next number in the sequence, he played the maximum coins. On the sixth and seventh pulls he played only one coin. On the eighth, thirteenth and twenty-first pulls he played the maximum coins. On all other pulls he played the minimum. He was sure that he would hit the big jackpot on one of the sequential numbers. He followed this system until the sequential numbers reached 21 and then started over since that number is so common in gaming and stretching the "theory" to 34 would be taking a "long shot." He claimed that the significant payouts usually occurred on the "right" numbers in the sequence.

We were fascinated and watched through several "rounds" of his system. He hit plums and oranges on a couple of "sequential" numbers and several cherries when he had only one coin in. Then he hit the big jackpot combination — with one coin in! Was he embarrassed! But he was not completely swayed from his theory. He rationalized the failure by saying he forgot to "purge" the machine of the previous player's patterns by playing the maximum coins for five or ten times first, to set it up for a "clean" Fibonacci sequence. Unfortunately for him, Fibonacci never programmed slot machines.

This is probably a good place to issue a warning about "systems" of slot playing. *No one has ever written a good "system," although many are advertised as "sure-fire" winning methods of play. Think about it! If anyone had such a system, he would be foolish to advertise it.* Those charletans selling "systems" are getting rich by marketing their theories, not by implementing them.

MISCONCEPTION #7:
If a floorman or mechanic opens your machine for any reason, it will stop paying.

This common complaint by players is unfounded. Floormen who open a machine to correct a "coin-in, time out" problem or to refill the machine when the hopper is empty, do not "flip a switch" to change the pay cycle or otherwise influence the program. They correct the problem with the coin acceptor or fill the hopper and then hit the "reset" button so that the machine can resume play. If there is any marked change in the pattern of payout, it could have occurred whether the machine had been opened or not. Although the interruption of your playing and any particular rhythm of play you had because the machine needed servicing might seem to cause a change in the pay cycle, that is not the case. *Since the Random Number Generator never stops, the appearance of a set of winning symbols or losing set of symbols has no direct correlation to the interruption of play, the opening of the machine, or the length of time between plays.* You could hit the big jackpot or go for a long time without hitting anything else. Some machines have even been known to repeat the big jackpot on the first or second play afterward.

Incidentally, it's a good idea to play off a jackpot because the odds of it repeating are the same as when you hit it the first time. If the machine pays the full amount of the jackpot, investing the maximum number of coins won't break you. Don't play a single coin on a multiple coin machine to "save" two or three coins, thinking it will probably not repeat. If it does repeat and you don't have the winning line lit or the maximum played for the bonus, you'll probably kick yourself all the way home.

If a player leaves a machine without playing off the jackpot, a floorman or other authorized casino employee will usually open the machine, take out a coin and play it off. Most players will avoid a machine showing a jackpot. So play off the jackpot, if for no other reason than courtesy. Also, depending on the type of machine, the playoff might give you a small return for your money. If a jackpot is paid by an attendent, you may be asked to play off the jackpot before you are paid. If you are out of change or refuse to do so, they'll pay you and then they

may play it off. But if they play and it "repeats" and you
don't get paid for the second jackpot, don't complain.

MISCONCEPTION #8:
**The higher the denomination of the machine, the higher
the payout.**
Not true, especially with large progressive jackpots.
All machines are programmed with a set theoretical per-
centage.

*Although the percentage of hold for the casino may be
less for the higher value machines, the random factor in
all of them is still the over-riding one.* You probably won't
play a single machine long enough to receive the total
theoretical payout percentage. Nor should you try to.
Ideally, you will catch it at the "right" time and play it
only while it is paying off.

MISCONCEPTION #9:
**If you win on nickels, move up to quarter machines.
If you win on quarters, move up to halves or dollars.**
This advice could ruin you. If you hit a royal flush for
$200 on a nickel machine, or a $50 jackpot on a nickel slot,
don't be tempted to "move up" to bigger and better wins
unless you are prepared to handle the additional risk.

*Remember that you can lose five times as much money
on quarters in the same amount of time, ten times as much
on halves and twenty times as much on dollars. Although
the possible win is usually proportionate to the investment,
it is certainly not guaranteed.*

We have found that most players have a favorite denomination that is most comfortable for them or suits their
entertainment budget. They play that type about 90

percent of the time with only an occasional experiment with higher denominations.

Quarter machines are by far the most popular throughout all casinos. The Las Vegas Sun stated that quarter machines accounted for 23% of Nevada's gambling take in a recent year and dollars accounted for 21%. Nickel machines and dollar machines rate almost equally in popularity, with fifty-cent machines rating third. Higher denomination types are limited and found mostly in the giant casino-hotels.

Experiment with all types first, within your means, and then settle down to the type that you feel comfortable playing, without a feeling of pressure that you have to win or else.

CHAPTER 6

Money Management

Do you have a household budget? Do you set aside a certain amount of your income for food, rent, utilities, automobile expenses, clothing, children's allowances, school expenses, and so on? If so, this part of money management should be easy for you. If you don't have a "budget" with a specific amount designated "entertainment," pay close attention! It's important.

We're going to outline some basic steps to try to keep you from going broke too soon.

Setting Limits

1. When you decide to go out to gamble, decide *before you leave home or your hotel room* how much you are going to take to spend for the evening, the day, the weekend, or period of time you plan to be gone.

2. Figure what the costs of the food, transportation, and other activities will be on your "trip," and put that amount in one pocket or section of your purse or wallet. *No matter what happens, don't dip into that pocket for "slot" money!*

3. Put the amount that's left in your "slot" pocket, that is, the section reserved for your gambling. If you're on vacation for a week, or more, try to plan each day's activities and "budget" your money accordingly. Keep only *one day's budget* in the "slot" pocket at a time, so you won't blow it all the first day and be tempted to spend funds reserved for other necessities and then have to cut the evening's entertainment or vacation short.

4. Next, let's assume you have read the entire book, know exactly where and what kind of slots you want to play, and have arrived at the casino. A good idea before you buy any change is to have a time limit in mind and a positive attitude that your money will "last" that long. Actually that statement may sound negative, but remember the objective is to win but at the same time realize that you may also lose.

Now, buy only enough change to last, say, for an hour. For example, if you plan to stay four hours playing quarter video poker and your stake for the session is $100, buy only $20 or $25 in change to start. Pick your machine and play.

5. *Don't play back any coins that drop in the tray.* Play only with your original buy. When that amount is played

out, stop playing and take stock. If the tray is full and/or runs over, shout "Hooray!" and fill up one of the coin buckets. If there are only a few piddling coins in the tray, put them in a cup anyway. Count your winnings before you buy any more change so you know whether you are ahead or behind.

Too many slot players will play the coins in the tray, whether it is full or almost empty, and continue to play until they are all gone. Their excuse is that they're trying for the big jackpot and will be content with nothing less. More often than not these losing sessions accumulate until one "big" win doesn't make up for the losses over a long period of time.

6. If you're ahead, cash in at the change booth and put the amount you're ahead—even if it is just a dollar or two —plus the original buy amount in an empty pocket or "winning section" of your purse or wallet.

7. Buy more change (if you are ahead) with another portion of the original stake and play that out, take stock again, cash in, etc.

8. If, after spending half of your stake, you are behind by that much or almost that much, revise your game plan. Change the type of machine you're playing to a lesser denomination, 3-coin instead of a 5-coin, a standard instead of a progressive type, etc. If you haven't done so before now, at least change machines. It's not a good idea to continue to "feed" a machine that doesn't pay anything.

9. On the other hand, if you're ahead and your machine keeps you ahead with each cash-in, keep playing. When your last cash-in amount is considerably less than the amount of stake spent, it's time to move on.

10. If the time you set to quit playing arrives and you

haven't spent all of your $100, consider yourself lucky. If you have spent it all and you have anywhere near that amount in your "winnings" pocket, consider yourself lucky also. A few dollars only indicates that you've had your evening's entertainment and the session was not a "total loss." If your winnings exceed your original stake, be happy! DON'T SPEND YOUR WINNINGS!

11. Now this is the toughest step of all. If you're out of time and you still have part of the original stake for the session left, put it in the "winnings" pocket. If the original stake is gone, don't dip into the "winnings" pocket whether it contains $2 or $200. DON'T PRESS YOUR LUCK *OR* YOUR LOSSES. THE SESSION IS OVER.

In his book, *Pay The Line*, John Gollehon gives excellent advice to craps and blackjack players that is appropriate for slot players or any gambler: "Winning must be reduced in your mind to its simplest terms—*if you have won any amount, you have not lost!* You must be content with a win of any amount." Further, he says, "Let small winning sessions accumulate . . . . You'll hit a big one from time to time, and more power to you!"

Don't be Greedy! According to Gollehon, "Greed makes losers out of winners." His opinion is: "Slot machines bring out the greed in players more than any other casino game." Before you take offense, consider his reasoning. The "big jackpots"—whether shown on a standard payout table or a super progressive display—"work on a player's greed" until they "give these machines all their money." Players "go strictly for the big jackpot which is virtually the same as going for broke!"

Whether or not we agree with Gollehon's opinion of slot players in general, suggestions and questions come to mind that might explain why slot players are more likely to be losers than table game players.

The lure of the big jackpot is definitely a factor. There is no posted "win" amount over a blackjack or craps table. Any projected or expected win figure has to be developed by the player himself who, if knowledgeable, will plan his betting strategy to achieve whatever goal he has in his own mind.

In contrast, the slot player's goal is influenced by the casino and is constantly before his eyes on the machine's pay table or the progressive jackpot display. It becomes a challenge to reach that goal, too often at any cost!

Say what you will about the competitive spirit of the gambler who tries to "beat the dealer" or "beat the odds" at the blackjack or craps table. He is more likely to quit after losing his stake than the slot player. He doesn't worry that someone else is going to sit in his chair after he leaves and win his money. But that's the way many slot players feel about giving up a machine they have "fed" tens or hundreds of dollars fruitlessly.

If another player hits the jackpot on the machine they have just left, they get angry, as if the player were winning *their* money... not the casino's money. If you can't stand to see anyone else win, don't hang around to watch someone else play after you've stopped. It can be disheartening, especially if you lost a sizeable amount. Losing is discouraging enough. Don't be a masochist and stick around for further agony.

Whether or not you follow these steps to the letter is unimportant. Develop your own discipline. That's the key word.

A disciplined player will resist the temptation to play more than he can afford to lose. A disciplined player's

winnings will bring more satisfaction in the long run, because his contribution has been more than a blind reliance on chance or luck. In a sense, he has "worked" at winning and had a good time doing it.

Credit

Although casinos extend credit to players, we do not recommend going into debt for "entertainment." Likewise, we recommend that you leave credit cards and bank automatic teller cards at home so you won't be tempted to use them in the all-too-convenient cash-dispensing machine available in all the large casino-hotels. Using these methods of exceeding your budgeted gambling stake could lead to regrets later. Besides, the interest or cash advance fee charged by the credit card companies also reduces the amount of your winnings and should be figured into your records.

Remember too, credit at a casino is like credit obtained from any other institution. You *do* have to pay it back; it is a legally collectable debt. Somehow, paying off a debt for a cash outlay for which you received no concrete benefit like a car, house, or TV set is very unpleasant.

Another "convenience" being installed at casinos is change machines. You can insert 5, 10, or 20 dollar bills and receive rolls of coins. These machines are replacing not only change booths which take up valuable slot space but also change girls. Personally, we have trouble getting the correct stamps or change from the automatic stamp dispensers at the post office and prefer not to use these change makers. Inserting more than one dollar in such a machine seems risky. Suppose it malfunctions, keeps your bills and doesn't give you coins. Then you have to flag down a change person or floorman anyway. This additional step in depersonalizing the casino and cutting down on the cost of personal service to increase casino profits should not be encouraged. If you run out of coins and don't want to give up the machine you're playing, press the button to turn on the light called a "candle" on top of the machine to alert the change girl that you need change or service.

Manage your time and money, and play with moderation and a great deal of discipline. And just as an athlete "psychs" himself into a winning frame of mind, the slot player should approach each session with a positive attitude also.

The IRS Tab

In the "old days," gamblers could choose to remain anonymous and insist on any win being paid on the spot, no questions asked. Now all casinos and gaming licensees are required to report any slot player's single win of $1,200 or more to the Internal Revenue Service. If you hit a jackpot of that size, a casino floor supervisor will ask you to complete and sign the form to report the win. You'll be asked for your driver's license or other ID and your social security number. The casinos also use this information to check their "files" for any credit markers or data on known felons or slot cheats.

If the jackpot is a sizeable one, they will probably ask to take your photograph with the machine, offering to send you a copy and perhaps free dinner tickets. If you choose to remain anonymous, they will refuse to release your name and photo to the press, or to display it in the casino along with their other big winners. *If you don't want to be bothered by salesmen, bunko artists or even thieves, remaining anonymous is a good idea.*

At the end of the year you will receive the Form W-2G from the casino reporting your win which you must attach to your annual tax return filed with the IRS. If you want to claim your gambling losses to offset the taxes assessed on your win, you may do so but you cannot claim any losses beyond your winnings, and you cannot carry losses forward from prior years.

Professional gamblers, however, who consider gambling their primary occupation or business can deduct other associated expenses allowable just as any other businessman. However, gambling losses cannot be deducted against other unrelated income.

A recent ruling by the U. S. Supreme Court involved the case of Robert Groetzinger who lost his job of 20 years with a truck company in Peoria, Illinois, and who started playing dog races full time in 1978. His winnings totalled $70,000 and he claimed losses of $72,032. He listed $2,032 as a business loss. The IRS claimed gambling was not a "trade or business," but the tax court ruled in Groetzinger's favor. The IRS took the case to the U. S. Court of Appeals who compared career gambling to playing the stock market and determined "full-time gambling for one's own account as a person's occupation or livelihood, and therefore as a trade or business."

The IRS then appealed to the highest court in the land. Five Supreme Court Justices agreed with Justice Harry Blackman's opinion: "If a taxpayer ... devotes his full-time activity to gambling, and it is his intended livelihood source, it would seem that basic concepts of fairness demand that his activity be regarded as a trade or business just as any other readily accepted activity.''

Keeping Records

For the non-professional as well as the professional gambler, the IRS may ask for proof of losses deducted.

Like Groetzinger, the professional gambler must keep thorough records of wins and losses and should expect to have them available for his tax preparer and the IRS if his return is audited.

For the novice, or occasional slot player, keeping records of money spent and won may seem like a chore and a bore. *Be assured that if you get lucky and hit the big one, you'll regret not having kept good records and documents to calculate your losses for deduction on your tax return.* Here are some suggestions:

Carry a pocket calendar and enter the amount spent and the amount won on the appropriate day you play. Also, include such data as where, what type of game played and, if possible, the name of slot or casino personnel from whom you bought change or perhaps who know you as a frequent player.

Another efficient record would be a small notebook to carry in your purse or pocket with a form to easily record the necessary data, i.e. with columns similar to the example on the next page.

DATE	TIME	PLACE	MACHINE TYPE	MACHINE NO.	AMOUNT SPENT	AMOUNT WON	NET LOSS	NET GAIN	WITNESSES/ COMMENTS

This chart is suitable for photo-copying

You can develop your own shorthand and abbreviations for the columns so that the entries are easy to make and easily interpreted. For instance, "CP" for Caesars Palace; "DI" for Desert Inn; "25VP" for quarter video poker; "13AB" for $1, 3-coin, any bar, etc. Don't try to rely on your memory to record everything when you get home.

Keeping a record has other advantages:

Noting the places and the machine numbers you play will provide a record of where you have the best luck and which machines consistently pay or, on the other hand, consistently take your money.

Some casinos announce the amount of large jackpots over their loudspeakers and often give the machine number hit. Take time to record these for future reference. You may want to play them later, especially if your records show that they hit frequently.

Your records may also help you to revise your future plans. The history over several months or trips may reveal significant patterns of play that you were completely unaware of before you kept records.

If you're a frequent player, the records may give you stark realization of your accumulating losses. In bits and pieces, your losses may not seem like much, but when you look at your "balance sheet" over several weeks or months, the numbers might change your whole outlook on slot machines. Then again, we can only hope that in many cases we didn't make the AMOUNT WON and NET GAIN columns wide enough for you to fit in all the zeroes!

Use the last column on our chart to also note comments on the day's events like: "Hit four-of-a-kind three times and played it all back." Later, it can make you think twice before repeating such folly. It could be abbreviated "4 X 3 = 0." If you hit a five-dollar jackpot six times and cashed in $10, it could be "$5 X 6 = $10." Not good math but good record keeping. If you cashed in the win, the other columns will reflect whether or not you bought more change and lost it all, had a winning session, or had an evening's entertainment for little or nothing.

Keep enough records to satisfy the IRS, but don't let the "chore" spoil your fun. One lady slot player interviewed on TV's "20/20" described detailed record keeping to the Nth degree. When she played, she recorded so much data it's a wonder she even took time to enjoy the game. Maybe she enjoys the record keeping more than the game.

Slot playing is supposed to be entertaining, and winning is definitely fun! But when it ceases to be fun, it's time to quit playing!

CHAPTER 7

Where To Play

Where is the best place to play slot machines? It's a difficult question to answer, but some information about the different places available and the type of machines found in each should be helpful to you.

In New Jersey, the only slot machines to play are in the resort hotel-casinos in Atlantic City. Gaming, other than the lottery, is illegal anywhere else in the state. Incidentally, casinos in Atlantic City are open from 10 a.m. until 4 a.m. on weekdays and 6 a.m. on Saturdays and Sundays.

But in Nevada, all casinos are open 24 hours every day. Part of the opening ceremony for many casinos is to cut the ribbon and throw away the keys. Many grocery stores, bars, and convenience stores are also open around the clock. There is always some place open for gambling in the larger towns and cities. You can play almost anywhere open to the public except churches, schools, major department stores, banks, federal buildings and most business offices. In almost every other business you will probably find one or more slot machines.

Let's categorize these gaming establishments, and make a few generalizations.

Supermarkets, Restaurants, Bars, Gas Stations, Etc.

As soon as you cross the state line into Nevada on a major highway or as soon as you enter the first town, you'll be able to find some place with slot machines to play. It may be only one old-fashioned mechanical reel-type machine still displaying lemons, cherries, bells and bars, or a more modern video slot, video poker, or video blackjack, depending on the age of the town, the business, or its owner. It may be in a one-gas-station wide-place-in-the-road, a new convenience grocery store, or a full-blown casino built to catch the "first chance" or "last chance" gambler, depending on which way you're going, or on which side of the highway it's built.

Usually these businesses, where gambling is only incidental to their primary activities, do not own the machines. The machines are placed there by licensed operators who have regular "routes" which they run daily, weekly, or less often, according to the amount of play the machines usually receive. These operators may be individuals with a

limited number of machines and locations, or they may
be one of the major manufacturers who takes advantage
of all opportunities to capture as much of the market as
possible. Routes are run in much the same way as your
usual vending machine routes.

If there are enough machines in the supermarket, restaurant, or bar, there may be a change person on duty to
sell you coins and pay out jackpots. If not, you may have
to get change from the cashier or manager of the business.
The same is true of a payoff for a jackpot not automatically paid by the machine. You may have to wait in line behind regular customers, which can really be a nuisance if
you're just passing through. If the cashier or the manager
cannot pay you the jackpot or service the machine if it
malfunctions, you could be in for a long wait while they
call the operator. Sometimes you can leave your name, address and phone number, and come back later to collect.
If you don't live in the neighborhood, are just stopping
for food, gas or car repairs, or a quick break, the delay
may not be worth the amount won.

Another danger in waiting for a machine to be fixed or
to collect your winnings is that you may get bored and pass
the time playing one or more of the other machines available. If your "gambling fever" is high, you might lose
money equal to or even more than what you've won. If
time is a factor, you're in a hurry, you have a business ap-
pointment to keep, your vacation is short, or you're bent
on a period of more serious gambling, pass by these
machines.

A better reason to ignore them is that most often in these
non-gaming establishments the machines pay less for
smaller hits even though the jackpot on an individual
machine may be comparable to that in some casinos. This

difference is seen more on video poker machines than on regular slot machines. Assuming you have wisely set aside the amount of money you intend to invest in slots, our advice is to save it for the casinos where the best odds or bigger returns for your investment are possible.

"Little" Casinos

The term "little" is relative. Here we refer primarily to the size of the establishment and the fact that it contains only slot machines, no table games. It may be adjacent to or include a souvenir shop since the majority of its customers are tourists, many on their first visit to the state.

On Fremont Street in downtown Las Vegas, commonly called "Glitter Gulch," you'll find a number of these "slot joints." They are also sandwiched between the larger casinos on the Las Vegas "Strip" which is Las Vegas Boulevard. Many more are found on side streets and in other parts of the city. In Reno, "The Biggest Little City in the World," little casinos are found throughout the city. These types also are common in the smaller cities of Nevada, such as Carson City, the state capital.

Characteristically, these slot joints have "open doors" to the sidewalk. Quite often attractive girls in mini-skirts or costumed creatures (clowns, animals, cowboys, etc.) stand at the doorway and hand out coupons for "freebies" to get you inside. The freebies may include drinks, souvenir key chains, miniature plastic slot machines, long distance telephone calls, drawings for "fabulous" prizes, candy, popcorn and free pulls on a special machine. These gimmicks usually have conditions. You have to register, show an out-of-state driver's license, or stick around for the drawing. They hope you'll play the machines while you're collecting the cheap freebies and waiting to win that "trip to Hawaii." The drawings do not always take place on schedule, if indeed a schedule is announced, so you can't leave and come back for the drawing. Naturally, you have to be present to collect the prize if you win.

These places are noisy. The space is limited and the music or hawking voices are loud enough to hear across the street or at least a block away. Inside, flashing lights, bells, whistles, and sirens go off when a jackpot is hit and even make some kind of noise with minor payouts, anything to give the impression that players are winning "lots" of money.

Sometimes they advertise that their machines "return up to 97%" of the money played. However, not all machines have the same percentage of return. Naturally the high percentage machines are not marked. If they were, few of the others would be played.

Most of these little slot joints are "tourist traps." Most "locals" avoid them. Fortunately, on the Strip and in downtown Las Vegas they are gradually being bought out by the larger establishments. But there will always be a few "die hards" as long as they can attract enough players. Unfortunately, these slot joints also attract the vagrants and bums because of the easy access to the street. Petty thieves jump at the chance to snatch a few coins from the tray of an unwary player. They can "hit and run" before the police or the security guards can be called into action.

In one joint a woman was playing at a bank of dollar machines near the door. She was playing five machines at a time and had coins in each tray. She hit the triple bars on the one nearest the street and moved down the line plunking coins in the others while the machine spit out

$150. As she reached the fifth machine in the row, a nondescript man walked over, grabbed two handfuls of the jackpot dollars, stuffed them in his jacket pockets and ran out the door. The woman screamed, but couldn't leave the rest of her machines to run after him. That would have been even more foolish. The thief may have had an accomplice waiting for her to do just that or any other dishonest person could have moved in on her machines. She was her own worst enemy. Had she played only one or two machines at a time, she could have protected her winnings. These small casinos do not have enough change girls to "watch" your machine while you "take a break" as in the larger casinos.

Even in the larger casinos, **it is not wise to play more machines than you can watch carefully.** Another lady was playing two quarter slots in a major hotel-casino and had quite a few coins in the tray along with two unopened rolls. She dropped a couple of quarters on the floor as she played the machine next to her. When she reached down to pick up the quarters, the man playing the machine on her other side quickly grabbed the unopened rolls and slipped away before she even realized they were missing. He was long gone before she could alert Security. She also could not describe him well enough for them to even know who to look for if he were still in the casino. There are lessons here for the novice slot player:

1. KEEP UNOPENED ROLLS IN YOUR POCKET OR PURSE AND DON'T PUT YOUR PURSE BETWEEN THE MACHINES. 2. KEEP YOUR EYES ON YOUR MACHINE (AND YOUR MONEY) AT ALL TIMES AND BE CAREFUL OF DISTRACTIONS. 3. TAKE A GOOD LOOK AT WHO IS PLAYING NEXT TO YOU. IF YOU GET A BAD

VIBE, MOVE AT ONCE. 4. DON'T TRY TO PLAY TOO MANY MACHINES AT A TIME. IT'S BEST TO PLAY ONE OR TWO AND THEN MOVE TO OTHERS AFTER YOU'VE HIT THE BIG ONE OR IF THEY'RE NOT PAYING.

Distractions can cost you money. One lady playing video poker next to her friend got so excited when the friend hit the royal flush that she forgot to pay attention to her own hand. She had a natural flush (7, 8, 9, 10, King of clubs) on the screen, with a possibility of a straight flush if she held four cards, threw away the King and drew the 6 or Jack of clubs. She not only forgot to draw for the straight flush, she forgot to hold the flush. She hit the draw button and got a garbage hand. She missed 30 coins for the sure winner already showing or a possible 250 coins for the straight flush. That's like slapping Lady Luck in the face!

Even some of the medium-sized and large casinos have open doors to the street with banks of noisy machines ringing and clinking to attract the "gambler" walking by with a few dollars burning a hole in his pocket. Security may be more effective in the larger establishments, with even a station close to the door, but these open doors still attract the petty thieves who haven't acquired the skill of the slick pickpocket who can work the crowd farther inside the casino.

Let's get back to the "little" casinos. One thing they have that you won't find in the larger casinos is penny slots. Some of the medium-sized casinos also have penny slots, and many new establishments include them at their grand openings, so there's something for everyone, at least in the beginning. When the casino gets enough regular trade, it phases out the penny slots and for two good reasons. They take up as much space as the other higher return machines, and they sometimes attract the bums, the pan handlers, and too many players who only spend $2 or $3 each.

If you want to play for fun and are not looking to make a killing on the slots, penny slots may be the answer. Although manufacturers make very few of them anymore, there are still some of the old mechanical types around. There are even a few of the modern progressive video jackpots to be won.

The Gold Spike casino on Ogden Street, one block off Fremont in downtown Las Vegas has a large selection of different types of penny slots. Several even have a top jackpot of one million pennies - that's $10,000!

At the Western Hotel and Bingo Parlor, a medium-sized casino hotel, just down the street from the El Cortez in Las Vegas, a little old lady was playing a penny slot that had a phenomenal $50,000 jackpot to be won. That's right! Dollars, not coins! Five pennies at a time to line up four sevens on the center line would win. She had been playing for hours and was tired. The machine was one of the credit types and she had 75 cents in credits. A man standing behind and watching her offered to pay for the credits. She readily accepted, not anxious to carry home 75 pennies. You guessed it! He hadn't even played off the 75 cents before winning the fifty grand. Ah yes! That's the stuff dreams are made of! I only hope the little lady had gone home and didn't read the announcement in the newspaper the next day. Of course, there was no guarantee that she would have hit the jackpot had she continued to play. We explained the reasons why in our opening chapter dealing with how the machines really work. Remember?

The Western is proud of its penny slot promotion. You

can see pictures of winners displayed on top of their two banks of progressive penny slots.

Fred Urich, Jr.	Watkins, CO	$13,005.20
Eugene Gozikowski	Las Vegas, NV	$95,172.50*
Raffaela Norstrum	Las Vegas, NV	$14,463.25
John Koch	Las Vegas, NV	$ 6,294.50

These jackpots were paid off all at once, not in installments over a number of years, as is the case for some of the huge progressive jackpots advertised.

As for the little casinos, on your first trip to Nevada, go ahead and collect the "freebies" if you want some cheap souvenirs to take home. But they may cost you more in coins lost in the low-pay machines than they would if you bought them in a gift shop. Remember, too, the cardinal rule for slot playing anywhere: THE MORE YOU PLAY, THE MORE YOU'LL PAY! Take a cue from the petty thief. HIT AND RUN!

Medium-sized Casinos and Slot Parlors

Again, the size is relative in this category. We will describe those establishments where the business is about half devoted to gambling and the other half devoted to some other activity such as a motel, RV park, restaurant, etc. This category also includes those casinos that have gaming as their primary activity but they are not large enough to have the volume of business enjoyed by the "giants" of the industry. They may have a few table games, but mostly slots.

*That's almost a hundred grand for five cents a play! For them, the three P's (patience, persistence, and pennies) paid off handsomely. Whatever their total investment, it couldn't have been anything near what they won.

Many have bingo parlors. Avid bingo players are usually avid slot players as well. Many spend the whole day and much of the night alternating between the bingo games and their favorite slot machine. Bingo players seem to prefer these casinos over the more glamorous giants, and you'll find more locals who regularly play there. These regulars have "favorite" machines and get upset when someone they don't know plays "their" machine.

Locals prefer these neighborhood casinos for a number of reasons. Perhaps they know the owners or managers and feel that they receive more personal or courteous service. They win more often there. They meet friends and enjoy the camaraderie as well as the gamble. They have "learned" which machines have the best percentage of payout and the best time to play when the casino is not so busy. They feel less intimidated than in the larger hotel-casinos. They like the food or the food prices and gambling is secondary (unless they're fooling themselves). They like to stay close to home or they have no car to go farther, and so on. Many of these reasons are valid and may even affect their "luck." (We'll explore the psychological aspect of playing in another chapter.) If you're visiting friends and they want to take you to their favorite hangout, by all means go. Good luck to you!

As for the slot machines in these places, you will find all kinds, old and new, and all types of pay tables from the best to the worst. Walk around and see what is offered and available before you play. If you find a bank of machines that is empty most of the time, chances are there is a good reason. Either they have been paying heavily and are on a cold streak, or their percentages are set so low that the players have learned to avoid them. You probably should avoid them also. You could test them. If they drop a few coins, keep playing. If they don't, walk away.

The Giants

They're glamorous! They're colossal! They're majestic!
They're palatial! They're phenomenal!

There aren't enough superlatives to describe these giants
of the gaming industry. In Atlantic City, in Reno, in
Tahoe, and above all in Las Vegas, the beauty, the wealth,
and the pleasure sought by millions of visitors annually
is found in these hotel-casinos.

Do you like castles, palaces, and imperial majesty?
You'll love Caesars Palace, the Imperial Palace, and the
majesty of Bally's or the Las Vegas Hilton. The Roman
motif at Caesars is carried out with a Cleopatra's barge
floating on the water (actually a cocktail lounge with live
entertainment) a Baccanal (gourmet restaurant), authen-
tic copies of Roman statues, a Circus Maximus (show
room), a Colosseum, a rotunda with a miniature Rome,
cocktail waitresses in mini-togas, beautiful fountains, marble columns, and art treasures (everything but a miniature
Vatican City). Caesars Palace has one of the most beautiful buildings and grounds of all the giants. John Stroup,
slot manager of the Flamingo Hilton, stated that Henri
Lewin of the Hilton wrote a letter to Caesars Palace,
thanking them for the beautiful view accorded the guests
of the Flamingo across the Strip.

At the Imperial Palace you'll find Japanese restaurants,
pagodas, torii's, cherry blossoms, Kobe steak house and
lovely oriental decor.

The desert motif (Las Vegas is in the desert) is found
at the Sahara, the Dunes, the Sands, the Desert Inn and

the Aladdin. Perhaps you prefer our western cattle country and Spanish heritage. If so, you'll like the Frontier, Sam's Town, Binion's Horseshoe, El Cortez and the Hacienda. You'll find the western mining theme at the Golden Nugget and in some medium sized casinos such as the Silver Nugget, Silver City, Gold Strike and Jerry's Nugget. The Golden Nugget in "Glitter Gulch" removed its former facade reminiscent of an old frontier saloon and it is now as classy as any hotel on the Strip.

Harold's Club in Reno features the "Silver Dollar Saloon" with a gun collection and museum, along with a scene-in-motion outdoor mural complete with a 33-foot waterfall and a pioneer's crackling campfire.

If you are a railroad buff, there are memorabilia of that vanishing industry found at the Union Plaza and Palace Station in Las Vegas, the Railroad Pass in Henderson, and in the Station House in Tonapah, Nevada, approximately 250 miles north of Las Vegas.

The tropical island motif is found, (where else?) at the Tropicana in both Las Vegas and in Atlantic City. The Trop in Vegas (everyone clips the names of the city and these well-known hotels) features a tropical island with the world's largest swimming pool, live flamingos, talking parrots, a weekly luau and swim-up blackjack tables.

Hotels which have borrowed heavily from the heritage of our neighboring state are the California, Barbary Coast, Golden Gate, Gold Coast and Fremont. For old-world enthusiasts there is the Riviera, Continental, and the Maxim. Don't forget the gambling theme; it's found at the Four Queens, Showboat, Holiday, Lady Luck, Fitz (formerly Sundance) and Paddlewheel. Binion's Horseshoe fits here too. The Four Queens also capitalizes on the "royal" motif.

The Nostalgia kick sweeping the nation is being manifested in the casino industry. Decor in new additions and renovations reflect the 50's and 60's with the popularity of automobiles that are now classics, and the music of the era played in lounges and in restored "juke boxes."

The Boyd group purchased the Stardust and remodeled it with a 50's and 60's theme. Ralph's diner is reminiscent of those "Happy Days." Their second floor addition to Sam's Town includes "Mary's Diner" complete with the remote coin operated juke boxes in each booth. The menu features a T-bone for 50 cents, but with meat it's $7.95. On slot machines, you can win restored automobiles of the era. A '57 Chevy was won on a quarter slot and was followed by a '66 red Mustang convertible.

In Reno, Eddie's Fabulous 50's opened recently with a rock 'n' roll theme from 10-cent popcorn and penny and nickel slots, and reruns of "Ozzie and Harriet" and "Howdy Doody." Cocktail waitresses, cashiers and dealers break out in song and do the "Twist."

Who says history doesn't repeat itself. Wonder if they'll go so far as to simulate the days when the "Mob" ran all the gaming establishments. We still hear old-timers reminisce about the "friendly" atmosphere of those "good old days" when owners didn't worry about making a profit in *all* departments. They were happy with the "take" from the games which more than made up for the losses on food and beverages.

The corporations running today's operations have already been showing losses in the food departments. The cheap buffets and coffee shops featuring $4.95 prime rib dinners have lines with waiting times of 30 minutes to an hour on holidays and weekends. Many residents find that dining out is cheaper than buying groceries! The late food specials feature complete breakfasts from 49 cents to $1.99 and New York steak dinners starting at $1.98. Nine out of ten customers will drive across town for a $1.98 steak and then drop $20 or more in the slot machines or at the tables.

The Colorado Belle in Laughlin (on the Colorado River southeast of Las Vegas) replicates a 608-foot-long 19th century three-deck Mississippi paddlewheeler complete with 209-foot-tall gold-crowned smokestacks and a 60,000 square foot casino. An adjacent six-story hotel is decorated in the style of old New Orleans. Built by Circus Circus, the Belle is adjacent to the Edgewater Hotel and Casino. The Belle opened with 1,200 slot machines, 44 blackjack tables, and two separate keno games as well as roulette, craps and live poker. It is claimed as the third largest casino in the world, quite an operation for this small river town growing by leaps and bounds.

The atmosphere or ambience in these giants varies with the decor, from formal and elegant to informal and neighborly. But strange as it may seem, you can be comfortable in blue jeans and boots at Caesars Palace and not feel out of place at Sam's Town in a tuxedo, formal and furs. Except for a few of the gourmet restaurants which require a coat and tie for dining, there is no dress code to gamble or even attend the shows. All the casinos really care about is that you have the money to play your game. Of course, they don't tolerate vagrants and pan handlers; they are quickly shown the back door by security guards. If you're clean and neat, you can wander around, soak up the atmosphere, and just watch the action, as long as you don't disturb the paying or playing customers. Take time on your first visit to appreciate the elegance of crystal chandeliers, rich furnishings, statuary, fine art and antiques found throughout most of these casino-hotels.

As for the slot machines, the giants carry the greatest variety and number and they carry the most progressive jackpots with hundreds of thousands to millions of dollars to be won, not to mention, automobiles, boats, and motor homes. Wander around and look them all over before you play. Again, there will be different pay tables, old and new machines and different special promotions. Don't be caught by the lure of the giant progressive jackpot closest to the door, but don't ignore it. It may be the best bet in the house. Just make sure that you know what to expect with any hit, small or large, and make sure that you collect all that is coming to you when you win.

Visit all these giants that your time permits. Then play where you feel most comfortable, or "lucky," or where you receive the most courteous service from the change person, the floorman, and the cocktail waitress. By the way, don't be confused by the title "cocktail waitress." She'll gladly bring you any beverage you like, be it milk, orange juice, soft drink, fruit juice or the more potent stuff. If you're gambling, drinks are free. Of course, it's polite to tip for the service, if the server was polite too.

On The High Seas

Do you want a "Rock and Reel" vacation? If so, you can rock to the waves and spin the reels on the many cruise ships offering gaming as well as the usual shipboard activities.

According to a recent Shipboard Gaming Guide, 29 cruise lines with 88 vessels offer both slots and table games on their cruises. A total of 4,337 slot machines are afloat, which equals approximately one fourth of the 18,198 slots reported for Atlantic City last year.

The Norwegian-Caribbean Lines (NCL) have six vessels which carry a total of over 500 slots. But the largest total, 653, can be played on the six ships of the Carnival Cruise Lines, operating out of Miami, Florida. The largest number on a single ship is 310 on NCL's *Norway*, the largest cruise ship afloat which accommodates 2,000 passengers. The *Azure Seas* of Admiral Cruise Lines carries 185 slots and its *Emerald Seas* has 145. The *Sovereign of the Seas* of Royal Carribean Cruise Line carries 175 machines. Princess Cruises of television's "Love Boat" fame operates five ships with a total of 368 machines. The *Royal Princess* offers 102 slots for diversion if your "love interest" doesn't materialize.

The cruise lines offering three to 14-day trips to various ports of call do not emphasize gaming in their advertising brochures. On the other hand, some lines offer one-day "cruises to nowhere" for the main purpose of gaming outside territorial waters. According to Michael Davis, in "Gaming & Wagering Business," shipboard gaming does not come under close scrutiny by regulatory bodies as land-based gaming does. However, he states that if shipboard gaming proliferates, "this free-floating industry segment might invite more stringent regulatory enforcement." If not, we can see that this proliferation could lend a whole new meaning to "piracy on the high seas."

Other Attractions

Many of the giants have added attractions that may or may not be related to gaming. The gift shops, the video arcades for the underage members of your party, the stage shows, the lounge shows, bowling alleys, spas, tennis, golf, and other special attractions keep the non-gambling members of your party occupied or provide a break from the gambling (if you're tired or on an unlucky streak). And, of course, there's always a swimming pool.

But there's a lot more that only Las Vegas could offer. Collections of antique slot machines, some silver and gold plated, are on display at the Maxim in Las Vegas and the Station House in Tonapah. The Stardust in Las Vegas includes a large museum devoted to Nevada's history of gambling and antique slot machines. Many other casinos also have a few non-playable antique machines for "historical color" usually placed near restaurants, change booths, or the cashier cage where players may have to wait in line for dinner or change.

The Imperial Palace has an antique automobile collection as well as more modern autos formerly owned by celebrities or more infamous people such as Al Capone and Adolph Hitler. Included is the 1962 bubble top Lincoln Continental ordered for President Kennedy and used by subsequent presidents and dignitaries such as the Johnsons and the Apollo 8 astronauts. To pique your interest, a few are displayed at various spots in the casino. The collection is rotated at various times throughout the year, so no two visits should be the same.

Many of these autos are periodically auctioned at this hotel to the highest bidder. At their auction recently, the highest price ever paid for an automobile was by Eric Traber of Switzerland for a completely restored 1930 Duesenberg for $1,150,000.00. A crowd of 7,500 bid a record-breaking $21,750,000 for 500 vehicles. John Madden, football coach turned sports broadcaster, bought a

1957 Ford Thunderbird for $27,000. Singer Kenny Rogers bought a 1957 Chevrolet convertible for $31,000. Michael Nesmith, formerly of the Monkees and founder of MTV, spent $26,000 for a 1957 Cadillac Brougham. (Incidentally, we heard that part of Nesmith's wealth comes from an invention by his mother. It is Liquid Paper, the fluid used to cover typing errors.)

Another large antique and famous-owner auto collection is an attraction of Harrah's Club in Reno, but it is housed in a separate facility about three miles from the hotel-casino.

Apparently, collectors are also gamblers. Recognizing this fact, the Sahara Hotel and also the Hacienda feature many "shows" in their own convention facilities for bottle collectors, weapons collectors, philatelists (stamp collectors), numismatists (coin collectors), lapidaries (rock collectors), doll collectors, antique collectors . . . you name it.

The Four Queens in downtown Las Vegas features Ripley's "Believe It Or Not." One magnificent display is the Matchstick London Tower Bridge made by Reg Pollard of Manchester, England. The model is 14 feet long, 4 feet wide and 5 feet 10 inches high. The project took 264,345 common matchsticks, 3 gallons and 5 pints of glue, 2 1/2 liters of varnish and 2,386 hours of labor. Laid end to end those matchsticks would be 6 miles long!

Binion's Horseshoe, which opened in 1951 in downtown Glitter Gulch, displays a million dollars in currency in a glass horseshoe and will take your photograph standing by it. We classify Binion's as one of the giants, although it is strictly a "gambling hall" with no show rooms, lounges, or swimming pool and only a small hotel with 80 modest rooms. "Lottery Players Magazine" quoted the

81-year-old Binion: "Let's put it this way. We got a little
joint and a big bankroll. All them others got a big joint
and a little bankroll." Binion's knows also that most
players like a good meal at a modest price. From 10:00
p.m. until 7:00 a.m. you can get a steak with baked potato,
salad and beverage for only $2.00. And it's good! Also to
accommodate its many customers, Binions built a second
high-rise parking garage a short block away from the main
facility.

The Golden Nugget displays the largest gold nugget in
the world. "The Hand of Faith" nugget was found near
Wedderburn, Victoria, Australia, in October 1980, and
weighs 875 troy ounces (61 pounds 11 ounces.) A man, his
wife, and four children were prospecting behind their
trailer and found it just six inches below the surface. It cost
the Golden Nugget a cool million. At current prices, the
gold alone is worth almost $400,000. Of course, the aes-
thetic value is more important. Prior to discovery of The
Hand of Faith, the largest gold nugget in the world was
the Robins Nugget also displayed at the casino. Weighing
189.7 troy ounces, the gold in the Robins Nugget is worth
only about $40,000. It was also found in Australia. Other
large nuggets from Alaska gold fields are also on display.

As you enter Las Vegas from the south on Highway 95
(Boulder Highway) you pass Sam's Town which features
a 56-lane bowling alley and a western dance hall where you
can learn to square dance. Further down the highway is
the Showboat with 106 bowling lanes. The El Rancho on
the Strip, Bally's in Reno, and the newly opened Showboat
in Atlantic City also have bowling lanes. The Gold Coast
is the latest casino to add bowling lanes in Las Vegas.

The casinos have found that bowling leagues get players
into their establishment two or three times a week. Many

bowlers like to play slots, so the machines are always close by. Bowling tournaments also bring in many out-of-towners during the non-tourist winter season.

The Professional Bowlers Association (PBA) holds annual tournaments at the two Showboat hotels each year. You can watch the top bowlers in the country competing on live television. In 1984, Sam's Town started its annual Ladies Professional Bowlers Tournament preceded by a one day Pro-Am No-Tap tournament. The amateurs bowl with the women pros and win prizes from $50.00 for fiftieth place up to $5,000.00 for first place.

Other non-gaming promotions by the hotels include championship boxing matches from Caesars Palace and the Las Vegas Hilton. The Nevada Resort Association figured that the Sugar Ray Leonard - Marvelous Marvin Hagler match in April 1987 brought in $100 million in revenue to Las Vegas. And don't forget the many celebrity golf and tennis tournaments held at the excellent courses and courts in Las Vegas.

Annual telethons raise millions for charity from the show rooms of these hotels. Such worthy causes as muscular dystrophy with Jerry Lewis on Labor Day and, in the spring, Easter Seals with Pat Boone and other celebrities attract many people who stand in line to contribute. While there, many of them also "contribute" to the casino profits at the tables and slot machines. Some believe that their "charity" will be rewarded with a "winfall," to coin a new word.

Bally's (formerly MGM) contains a movie theater which runs old-time classics such as "Gone With The Wind." The live MGM lion was prominently stationed in the theater lobby and was a favorite of tourists and locals alike. Upstairs, a long hall was lined with portraits and marble busts of MGM's most famous movie stars. When Bally's bought the MGM, the lion had to go. Ironically, Bally Manufacturing used to be known as Lion Manufacturing Company. Some people speculated whether or not they would consider changing their name back again so they wouldn't have to get rid of the lion motif prominent in the hotel and casino. They didn't!

Caesars Palace also contains a movie theater called the OMNIMAX. This special theater shows movies in the "round." The newest hotel with movie theaters is the Gold Coast Hotel and Casino located on West Flamingo Road.

Circus Circus on the Las Vegas Strip, features (what else?) free circus acts thirteen hours every day including acrobats, high wire and trapeze artists, dog shows, unicyclists and much more. A Las Vegas Sun article recently featured the hotel's Director of Entertainment, Mike Hartzell, who "performs an uncommon dual role as department head and as senior ringmaster for the world's largest permanent circus." Hartzell made his first professional circus appearance when he was three weeks old, in his mother's arms, riding on an elephant. "As ringmaster, Hartzell is easily accessible to the public, and he serves as a one-man information bureau, coping with the sublime, the ridiculous and the unexpected...." At various times he has had "to babysit, to make change, to locate wandering husbands and to explain casino games."

In addition to the circus attractions, this family-oriented casino circles the main casino with a second story carnival "midway" complete with coin toss, water balloons, milk bottle game and almost every other game imaginable for the "kiddies" to enjoy while Mom and Dad gamble. Make no mistake, these carnival games are not free. They make a "bundle" for the casino. As one famous comedian put it, he spent $50.00 trying to win a stuffed animal he could have bought in the gift shop for $13.95. But playing is more fun for the kiddies as well as the adults. It's "winning" that provides the thrill, not just the prize.

The success of the carnival attractions at Circus Circus is reflected in their expansion. In order to make way for more slot machines, they eliminated most of the beautiful water fountains in front of the building. They also used space formerly occupied by gift shops to add a "West Casino" and built a motel "Manor" along with an adjacent RV park. Next came a "Skyrise" hotel and garage. The Manor and Skyrise are linked to the Main casino with an elevated shuttle system and a walk-way. The Manor has a small lobby that is filled with slots, while the Skyrise contains a small casino with lots of slots and Circus Circus' new Race and Sports Book.

These giant hotels contain gift shops with everything from inexpensive souvenirs and paperback books (including this one, hopefully) to designer clothes, jewelry, furs, antiques and art. However, many of the casinos are shrinking the space allowed for these stores so that additional slots can be added. Slots guarantee a greater return per square foot.

Other attractions a short distance from Las Vegas are Hoover Dam on the Colorado River which formed Lake Mead with its fishing, boating, water skiing, and breathtaking scenery. The dam built in the 1930's was a project of the Work Projects Administrations (WPA) and provided employment during the depression days. Las Vegas was merely a railroad station with a few saloons, hotels, and gambling halls downtown in those days.

You can take West Charleston Boulevard to the Red Rock Canyon area where amateur archeologists can

examine ancient Indian petroglyphs or where you can pic-
nic and attend an open-air production of a Shakespeare
play on a summer evening.

Approximately 30 miles to the northeast is Mount
Charleston for camping and hiking in the summer and Lee
Canyon for skiing in the winter. Of course, you can't find
better skiing closer to casinos than at Lake Tahoe and
Reno where you can enjoy 18 downhill areas and 10 cross
country tracks.

Also near Reno is Virginia City where Mark Twain
wrote many of his famous tales. The museum of old mining tools and equipment and display of the location, depth
and facts about the mines in that area is both interesting
and educational.

Are you an autograph hound? Do you want to see celebrities "off stage?" Besides seeing them "live" in the hotel
show rooms, you might even rub shoulders with them in
the casinos or restaurants around town.

Players interviewed report:

"I watched Jimmy Dean play blackjack at the Landmark."

"I got Liberace's autograph on a flight from Los
Angeles to Las Vegas."

"I saw Andy Williams leaving Caesars Palace as I was
going in and he smiled at me!"

"In the coffee shop at the Landmark our table was right
next to the one where Dottie West was eating lunch."

"I've played the 50 cent slot machines side by side with
Redd Foxx many times at Sam's Town."

"I was once eyeball to eyeball with "Wilt the Stilt"
Chamberlain at Caesars Palace. That's not easy since I'm
only five-two and he's over seven feet. I was on the upper
sidewalk and he came toward me walking on the lower

sidewalk. When I recognized him, he said 'hello' and waved.''

"We chatted with Mike Farrell (B.J. in M*A*S*H) while standing behind him in the Sunday Brunch line at the MGM Grand.''

"I once sat across the aisle from Phil Harris on a flight from St. Louis to Las Vegas. You know, they had over-booked the flight and someone else had the same seat assignment as his. They made a big stink about it to the flight attendant but Phil was very gracious and moved to another seat. He also signed autographs throughout the flight without complaining. And come to think of it, I don't think he drank any hard stuff either. Later, at the baggage claim, he even carried his own luggage.''

If you're still not sure where to play slots, at least you should have some idea what else you can do with your time and money. We only hope you spend *both* wisely.

CHAPTER 8

Cheating: Methods and Consequences

No book about slot machines would be complete without some reports of slot cheating and its impact on the industry. Stories of "rigged" jackpots receive sensational coverage in the newspapers. Players worry about casinos "rigging" the machines so they won't pay. Casinos worry about dishonest employees and crooked "players." And residents of non-gaming states get a distorted image of the whole industry. To set the record straight, let's look at the problem from all sides and put it in the proper perspective.

Trying to cheat the machines is risky business, even if you're not "in" the business. The story that follows is a good example.

This portly Polish gentleman in a not-so-fashionable blue suit, shiny with age, walks up to a bank of slot machines. Veteran players are plunking in five coins at a time and nothing is dropping in their trays. The newcomer plays one coin at a time and gets an occasional return on two or three cherries and hits three plums. After exchanging glances, the players beside him can't contain their irritation any longer.

"Why don't you play the max?" says the gentleman on his right.

"The max?"

"Yes, the limit," explains the lady on his left. "If you hit the three sevens with only one coin, you don't get the big jackpot." She points to the pay table on the glass and explains the added bonus for playing the limit.

"Ah!" So the Pole starts playing five coins at a time.

After about fifteen minutes none of them are hitting more than a few cherries and plums. They each buy two more rolls of coins. The change girl pats each man on the shoulder and wishes him luck. She turns to the lady and smiles, "Hit the big one, Honey!"

"These machines are really tight tonight," replies the lady.

"They sure have 'em screwed down," agrees the man. "We've gotta loosen 'em up. They're so tight they squeak!"

The machine responds on cue with its built-in noisemaker chirping like R2D2.

The Polish gent pauses, hand at the coin slot, looking from one veteran to the other, brow wrinkled. His literal understanding of English tries to comprehend this idiomatic dialogue. Suddenly, the figurative light bulb goes on over his head!

"I come right back." He scoops up the few coins in the tray and runs toward the door.

"I'll hold your machine," says the lady, placing a coin cup over the machine handle and stuffing another one in the tray.

About five minutes later the Pole returns, slightly winded.

"I fix. I make it loose!" He holds up a can of WD-40. "I keep it in my car. Good stuff!" He pokes the red tube down the slot of his machine.

"Hey, what're you doin'?" shouts the man, backing away.

"Good grief!" adds the lady. "You can't do that!"

Before they can explain further, the Pole has emptied the whole can into the machine! He steps back smiling, proud of his handiwork. He reaches into his coat pocket for a coin and drops it in the slot.

WHOOM! Surrounding players gather at the machine. Security guards converge, 10-4ing into their walkie-talkies. No one knows for sure if the spray-oil made the machine any more "loose," but one thing is for sure. Slot machines are not supposed to smoke!

Slot Cheating Rings

One of the members of a highly publicized slot cheating ring testified in court for more than four days, revealing many of the methods and devices by which such rings are successful in ripping off the casinos and the public. Gaming authorities, casino managers and slot manufacturers were amazed at his descriptions of how easy it was to cheat the machines. He described how the ring recruits "collectors" for their rigged machines from among ordinary "citizens" who have no record of illegal activities or brushes with the law. In fact, he too was recruited as a collector by members of the gang and earned enough money collecting illegal jackpots to pay his way through slot mechanic school.

While in mechanic's school he had a slot machine at home that he practiced rigging and finding different ways to cheat. He taught himself how to pick locks and to duplicate keys to machines. He could use a probe to find the combination of grooves in the lock and then make a key to fit. After just looking at a key, he could duplicate it. One way to see the key was to jam a particular machine in a casino. Then when a player called a floorman after losing money in the slot, he would stand close enough to get a good look at the key.

Later, he drilled holes in the side of a machine and used a wire to manipulate the machine into hitting the jackpot. Once he got his wire caught in a machine at Caesars Palace. The group watched the machine while he went next door to a gas station to get a pair of pliers to either pull out the wire or shove it all the way in. They guarded the machine for 15 minutes before he got back. The pliers didn't help and they finally abandoned the machine with the wire still sticking halfway out!

He described the role that each member of the group played in their operation. There was a "general manager" who decided which machines to hit and who would be there for the operation and sometimes arranged for the collector. There were those who acted as "lookouts," scouting for likely machines to hit. And there were "blockers" to conceal the actual rigging from casino employees and security guards by surrounding the machine or standing in the way of the concealed cameras when trained at the machine.

On his second day of testimony, the accused cheater demonstrated his techniques by rigging three different Bally electro-mechanical quarter machines for jackpots. The first machine took eight seconds; the second took 24 seconds, and the third just under a minute. He apologized for taking so long because he was "out of practice" after spending four months in prison.

In each case the rigging involved stopping the clock—the wheel device that controls the spin and stops the reels. After stopping the clock, he could align the reels where he wanted them and then free the clock to record the jackpot. He explained how a magnet could be placed near a spot where the electronic components of a machine were located and "put the machine to sleep" so that its built-in security systems would not work.

This successful slot cheat earned about $600,000 a year, which was about one fifth of the approximately $3 million a year collected by the ring. But, easy come, easy go! He said he had squandered the money he "earned." At the time he was sentenced, he claimed he had only about $10,000 and his house left.

Black Boxes

Rumors indicate that electronic "black boxes" have been used by slot cheats to rig jackpots in the new microprocessor controlled machines. Such a device could be produced; however, none have ever been found by gaming authorities.

One ingenious cheater did develop a tiny radio receiver to fit inside the hopper microswitch—the device that counts how many coins the machine pays. He recruited slot mechanics in the casinos to install the receivers, paying them $500.00 for each. Then he played the machines until he hit a jackpot. During the payout he would "light-up" a fake cigar which contained the tiny transmitter to instruct the receiver to deactivate the microswitch. The machine would dump all its coins without counting them. He "smoked" out a whole bunch of jackpots before getting caught. The gaming board confiscated many of the receivers and the "expensive" stogie. Whether or not any machines out there are still waiting for that "loaded" cigar is anyone's guess.

It has been estimated that there are about 120 ways to cheat an electro-mechanical slot. Most manufacturers and operators have modified the machines to eliminate most of them, but for the record let's describe the most common methods of cheating that have been used.

Slugging

"Slugging" is using a counterfeit or foreign coin instead of a legal coin or token to play the machines.

Gaming Authorities were perturbed a few years ago when a government contractor at the Nevada Test Site sold surplus washers at one of their periodic property disposal sales. The washers were the exact size, weight, and thickness as quarters, halves, and dollars. Several purchasers packaged and sold them in rolls like coins. Not surprisingly, they showed up in gaming devices all over town.

The Gaming Control Board eventually made sure that such washers were disposed of somewhere *other than* Nevada.

Recently, two Las Vegas women were arrested for slugging slot machines. Later, authorities obtained search warrants and found nearly 500 slugs and special manufacturing equipment in their apartment!

The use of foreign coins in slots is also a major problem. Barney Vinson, in *Las Vegas Behind the Tables,* relates the incident of the cheater who was apprehended for using foreign coins in the machines. He had 10,000 in his car and had already dropped 90,000 of them into the machines before being arrested.

The Mexican peso is about the same size as a quarter and often works in quarter slots. Canadian quarters sometimes get mixed in with U.S. coins in the rolls you buy or in the hopper fill. They will come out of the hopper with your winnings, but they'll jam the coin acceptor if you try to play them back. If you receive one during payout, the change girls will generally exchange it for you.

Stringing

One method of free-playing a machine is stringing. As the name suggests it involves working the same coin up and down in the coin acceptor by attaching a string or thin flexible wire.

For instance, we happened to play a video poker machine once that another player had just left. After a few plays we hit a flush for a small win. The machine paid about half of the winning amount and stopped. We were seated at an adjacent machine and had been playing it before reaching over and playing the one that jammed. We called an attendant who opened the machine to check the hopper. The floorman asked who had been playing the machine before we did, and we described the old, thin fellow with spectacles who had just left. He then called security, cleared the jam, and held up a quarter with a nylon thread tied through a tiny hole near one edge.

The old guy had been "stringing" the machine and had left when the thread broke. The floorman dumped the whole hopper of coins into the tray and went through it looking for any other strings or slugs. The security guards alerted the rest of their force to look for the old man, but he had left the casino. Most cheats knowing a slug or stringed coin is inside do not risk calling attention to themselves by asking a floorman to fix a machine. We were paid and not accused of cheating, probably because the change girl remembered selling us coins a few minutes before.

Spooning

Although some players caress their machines and coo at them like lovers, that's certainly not illegal and not the kind of spooning we're talking about.

Spooning was a method of cheating the old mechanical machines which is no longer a problem with the electro-mechanical and microprocessor-controlled units. The old mechanism for payout included a series of slides which moved backward and forward under the coin tubes. Each slide as it moved backward would allow a coin to pass through to the payout chute into the tray below. If a jackpot was two or more coins, that many slides were used. A spoon shaped device could be inserted from the bottom of the machine through the payout chute to hold all the slides back when a jackpot was hit. The entire contents of the coin tube would then dump into the payout tray.

To foil these spooners, manufacturers first installed a series of right angle "gates" in the coin chute to prevent spooning. Later the electro-mechanical machines included a hopper to replace the old coin tube/slide combination. The new payout mechanism in the hopper design could not be cheated by spooning.

Rhythm Method

The Rhythm method of play, while not exactly illegal, was another way slot players could consistently win on the old machines. Widely used in 1948 through 1950, cheating by this method was responsible for a significant drop in slot revenue. Since the machine mechanism was not tampered with, casinos were baffled when machines began to pay more often than usual.

A timing mechanism that determined the length of time the reels spin had from seven to eight seconds after the last reel stopped before it went dead. During those few seconds, each machine had a "hold" count which varied from five to 25. By pulling the handle at the exact hold count, the player could line up the reel on the same symbol as before.

The rhythm player first memorized the positions of the symbols on the reels. Then once the desired symbol appeared on the last reel, hold-count could be determined after a few trial plays by counting a number in the five to 25 range and determining how many places away the winning symbol was from the pay line. They then decreased the count by the number of places the winning symbol was

down from the center line or increased it by the number
it was up from the center line. When the exact hold-count
was determined, they easily counted to that number and
pulled the handle before the clock went dead to keep lining up the winning symbols.

*Rhythm players became so skillful they could manipu-
late all three reels. Some even held schools to teach the
method and sold pamphlets explaining the system.*

To combat rhythm players, manufacturers installed
variators. One form of variator was an extra gear on the
third reel to vary its stopping time, thereby thwarting
players who consistently won by timing their play. One of
the first machines with a variator was the Jennings' "Tic
Tac Toe" model introduced in 1951.

A reformed rhythm player, who has been working at
various casinos in Las Vegas, received approval from the
gaming control board as a key employee after his promotion to slot manager at a large casino. His boss indicated
to the authorities that he had been running the operation
and would continue to do so.

Another admitted slot cheat we know was a respected
employee of a small manufacturing company in Las Vegas
and has also worked for various casinos in the city.

Think about it. These reformed cheaters make excellent
slot managers; they know who and what to watch out for
to protect their employers.

Handle Manipulation

Both mechanical and electro-mechanical machines
which were out of adjustment could be cheated by
manipulating the handle pull.

One way was called "walking the reels." If the handle was pulled forward in a rather slow jerky manner, it would jerk the reels a few places at a time instead of giving them the normal "free" spin. A few pulls could jockey the winning symbols into a payout position.

Another way was a quick, hard jerk of the handle after a previous win. As a result, the reels sometimes would not spin at all and the dumb machine would pay again.

A third method was to squeeze the handle as close to the cabinet as possible as you pulled it, which would allow you to "free play" the machine.

Players often broke machine handles using these tactics. But handle manipulation was risky. Casino employees or security guards would watch you carefully, and if caught manipulating a handle in any strange way, they would show you the door or call the authorities.

Handle manipulation faded from the scene when electro-mechanical and microprocessor machines became more sophisticated. The handle pull was no longer the triggering device for the reel spin. It was useless. It was retained and is still a part of the action because players resist change and expect a slot machine to have a handle to pull. Early computerized units without handles got very little play. Those with a handle that did not simulate the "clicking" sound of the old mechanicals also were avoided by players.

Inside Cheating

The problem of cheating is not confined to "outside" rings or independent operators. Nowhere else do you find such large amounts of money being handled in plain sight

24 hours a day as in the casinos (except at the U.S. Mint). The constant sight of thousands of dollars changing hands can be a strong temptation to a change person with a family to support, a cashier who might have staggering hospital bills, or even a slot manager who likes to "live high on the hog." Casinos constantly watch their employees to prevent theft. In the old days, casino owners and managers dispensed their own "justice" to dishonest employees. They were fired and sometimes encouraged by more drastic means never to steal again.

Slot managers used to be the top link in the security chain, responsible for surveillance of employees and verification of slot jackpots. But position does not always guarantee integrity. One slot manager succumbed to the temptation and decided to take an extra "commission." Since he only made large jackpot payouts, he was able to conceal his embezzlement for five years.

He would write out the tickets for a jackpot, get the money from the cashier and pay the lucky winner. Every day about five o'clock, he wrote a ticket recording a $500 jackpot and pocketed the money. A conservative calculation of 5 days per week (slot managers often work six or seven) times 52 weeks per year, times $500 comes to about $130,000 per year ($650,000 over five years).

How he was discovered, or by whom, is a mystery, but he literally "disappeared." He may be "retired" in a plush resort in Mexico or he may be "resting his bones" somewhere in the desert around Las Vegas.

Now, Nevada Gaming Control Board Regulations require casinos to establish internal controls acceptable to the Board. Casinos must describe all internal methods of preventing illegal activities during receipt and accounting of money, credit extended (markers), payment of jackpots, etc. Once approved by the Board, these controls must be strictly followed by the casinos. Gaming authorities perform undercover surveillance as well as frequent audits to assure that the state's and the public's interests are protected.

Controls usually include witnessing of jackpot payouts and hopper refills by two or three employees who sign or initial the ticket recording them. You will see this procedure if you hit a jackpot or your machine runs out of money. New computerized tracking systems are also being developed and installed by casinos to monitor the action on each machine.

One owner of a small casino frequently disguised herself as a change girl and worked throughout the casino looking for slot cheats or dishonest employees. When she spotted a slot cheat, she notified authorities to come in and make the arrest. When she discovered an employee sampling the take or a slot mechanic "rigging" a machine, she went upstairs, redressed in her owner's attire, returned and fired the employee. This method was quite effective for her small operation.

Gaming authorities would like casinos to report these dishonest employees for prosecution. Merely firing them leaves them free to find work in other establishments with another opportunity to steal. Authorities would also like to see their sheriff's "work cards" confiscated so they could no longer work in a casino. In case you didn't know, all employees are required to obtain a "work card" from the sheriff's office before being allowed to work in a gaming establishment, whether they work in the casino, at the hotel administrative office, or as a custodian, maid, or maintenance person. However, proper incentives for casinos to report the "bad apples" have not been devised. It is easier and less expensive to fire an employee than to prove in court that he was stealing. Why should casinos bother prosecuting if there is little or no chance of obtaining restitution? And business is business. One casino doesn't often deliberately try to help its competitors.

Before you get the impression that all the casinos and their employees are "out to get you and your money" by any means possible, remember that most of these people are hard working ordinary people like the rest of us, trying to make an honest living. For instance, Anita Dixon, a maid at the Imperial Palace, was cleaning a room, and as she took off a pillow case, an envelope fell out. It contained $2,165.00 in cash! She was shocked and scared. She called the housekeeping office who sent a security officer to get the money. The hotel traced the owner through guest records and returned the funds. In appreciation for her honesty, Anita and her husband were treated to a dinner in the hotel's gourmet restaurant.

Impact of Cheating

It has been estimated that Nevada casinos lose at least 20 million dollars to cheaters each year. Figures cited at a recent gaming conference in Reno were even more staggering. A known group of cheaters, expected to be charged, was collecting an estimated $600,000 per day and sometimes as high as $1 million a day in illegal gambling.

Slot cheats deprive honest players and gamblers of the opportunity to hit the large jackpots, not to mention the money they spend in play that increases the size of those jackpots. Remember, the casinos place a portion of each day's "take" or "drop" on these machines into an "escrow" account for the purpose of meeting the big payoff when the jackpot is hit. If it is hit too frequently by cheaters, the casino, like any other business, will "build" the losses into the price of their products—jackpots. The "price" is the percentage you pay.

At a recent International Gaming Exposition, Chief Deputy Attorney General Dan Reaser of the Gaming Division in Nevada described the extent and impact of slot machine cheating. Some of the statistics he cited are astounding.

For instance, licensees in Nevada were recently asked to turn in the slugs they had taken from their machines. Only 25 percent of them responded, turning in seven and one-half tons of slugs! The next year nine tons were received! This quantity of slugs represented from five to six million dollars lost to slot cheats for slugging alone. Can you imagine how much money was really lost to slot cheats if you consider all the casinos that didn't respond?

Why didn't all the casinos turn in the slugs and foreign coins? Because they are taxed on the revenue, whether the coins received are phony or foreign. As an incentive for casinos to turn in these illegal "coins," the Nevada legislature was considering a tax exemption for casinos on these bogus coins if surrendered.

Deterrents to Cheating

CAN THE MANUFACTURERS DEVELOP A CHEAT-PROOF SLOT MACHINE?

The answer is "No." Whatever one man can do,

another man can *un*do. As one casino owner said about the purpose of a slot machine lock, "It's to keep honest people honest and keep the door from flying open and hitting you in the butt as you walk by."

However, manufacturers do try to develop cheat-proof machines. They now install timers in slot machines that clock each coin as it goes out. If a coin does not go out every six to eight seconds during a payout, the machine locks up and payout stops. The timer also locks up the machine if the switch is open too long, coins get jammed in the hopper, or someone inserts a wire to hold the switch open.

To counteract machines being cheated with magnets, casinos install reed switches and relays that "black out" the machine if a magnet is placed close to the cabinet. A former Gaming Control Board employee relates how one day a woman with a very large purse walked down the aisle between two rows of machines. She left a path of blacked out machines on both sides from one door to another, with security guards hot on her heels! That must have startled a few players! The magnet had to weigh at least 14 pounds to affect machines at that distance. Maybe she had plans to "attract" a Big Bertha jackpot.

In another incident a man had a magnet disguised as a roll of lifesavers in his coat pocket. As he walked past a row of slots, his coat floated toward the machines. Security guards had a good laugh about that one too.

You might wonder why they weren't arrested. It's not illegal to carry a magnet. But it is certainly illegal to try to use it to cheat a machine.

Even though casinos added these safeguards, they did not always help, as in the case of the slot mechanic working for the casino, who kept disconnecting the relay. When asked why, he replied, "Because it kept blacking out the machine!" Was he really that naive or was he also cheating the machines?

This brings to mind another incident of a casino being its own worst enemy. The casino had installed some promotional signs on top of its machines. Later, it removed the signs and forgot about the screw holes which were left open. Cheaters found that by inserting a drinking straw down the holes, they could trip the odds unit and repeatedly free-play the machines without inserting any coins.

Russ Scott, a long time employee at various casinos, tells us that about 20 years ago the Gaming Control Board held a school to educate casino and manufacturing personnel on the methods used by slot cheats. Suddenly, the cheating incidents escalated, so the school was discontinued.

Scott also related a story about a team of slot cheaters who used to drill holes in the sides of slot machines. The holes were then filled with plastic wood. Later, another guy came along, tapped out the plug and inserted a wire to set up the reels for a jackpot. This method of cheating is no longer effective since most of the mechanical reel machines have been replaced with microprocessor controlled machines.

There will probably never be a machine that cannot be tampered with in some way to collect an illegal jackpot. However, a higher degree of technical knowledge is necessary to tamper with the microprocessor designs. On the other hand, casinos and the gaming regulatory bodies don't always have the personnel who keep up with the "state of the art" or who have the expertise to determine absolutely *how* or *if* a machine has been cheated. Manufacturers continue to build in safeguards, but they are kept "top secret." Industrial espionage and reverse engineering are real threats to their operations. Spies from the cheating rings, surveillance experts from regulatory agencies, and possibly spies engaged by the casinos could infiltrate a manufacturer's operations.

For that matter, engineers very often get a "better offer" from a rival manufacturer. We know of instances where some employees are paid an excellent salary (an offer they can't refuse?) and are tied up by contract for a number of years, whether they continue to produce or not, only because of what they "know" about a manufacturer's machine. Such an arrangement could be enviable for someone who is content to "have it made." But an inventive engineer who finds satisfaction in what he can create might find this situation restrictive, boring, stifling, or intolerable.

CAN COMPUTER AND ELECTRONIC ENGINEERS DEVELOP A COIN ACCEPTOR THAT WILL REJECT SLUGS AND WASHERS?

Electronic coin acceptors which will reject bogus coins are available. However, these acceptors are expensive to produce and sell for $40 to $50 each as compared to the old "reliable" mechanical acceptor that costs $7 or $8. Because of the ever-increasing competition between manufacturers, they try to sell machines as cheaply as possible.

One exception is with the dollar slots. Due to the weight of the silver dollars or tokens, the regular coin acceptors have a short life and must be replaced more often. Further, counterfeit dollars could really eat a big hole in the casino's profit, especially with the giant progressive jackpots now offered. And let's face it, if you had a hefty

supply of counterfeit coins, which machine would you
play? One with a jackpot of $1,000 or a *quarter of a million
dollars?* By the way, that question was not a recommen-
dation to try to use slugs, washers or any other substitute
for legal coins. It was merely a hypothetical question to
illustrate the logic used by slot operators worried about
sluggers.

Now, let's examine that logic a little closer. If you were
"slugging" a machine, would you take a chance on hitting a huge jackpot and have the stamina to undergo the
"third degree" by casino management and their security
if they opened the machine and found counterfeit coins
in the hopper? Not only would you probably not get paid,
you might be arrested. Even if you were "clean" (no bogus
coins on your person) they might not believe you. Even
if the good coins outnumbered the bad ones by a hundred
to one, they still might not believe you. Only in court or
on the official arrest record are you "presumed innocent
until proven guilty." Also, some casino security guards
are not known for their diplomacy or "soft touch" in dealing with suspected cheaters or thieves.

A slugger with any common sense would stick to machines that have jackpots automatically paid by the
machine. That's one reason you will find very few machines that automatically pay a jackpot of $1,000 or more.
Larger jackpots are paid by an attendant, and the payoff
is witnessed in accordance with the procedure approved
by the Gaming Control Board for that particular casino.

Also, sluggers face another problem. If the slugs jam
the hopper during payout by a machine, the floorman will
discover it when he opens the machine. So smart sluggers
do not "fill" a machine with slugs because they would get
them back in a reduced payout. Or if the hopper jammed

during payout, they might have to abandon the machine before it is opened for fear of being caught.

CAN THE CASINO VERIFY THAT A JACKPOT IS LEGITIMATE ON THE NEW MICROPROCESSOR-CONTROLLED MACHINES?

Yes. If you hit a large jackpot that the casino feels should be verified, you may see them check the machine's memory chips in a small box called a "memory comparator." Master memory EPROMS for the machines are locked up and under tight security. (EPROM stands for "erasable electronically programmed read only memory.") The master EPROM is brought out and placed in the box beside the one from the machine being tested. A lighted "yes" or "no" indicates whether or not the memories match. If they don't match, you could be in big trouble, in danger of being arrested for cheating.

IGT originally developed the comparator in 1980 when casinos were becoming paranoid that cheaters could be substituting EPROMS. It was developed for use on 3 voltage EPROMS and in IGT's machines, but it did not work on the popular Bally E-Series slots, which used single voltage EPROMS, nor did it work on machines made by A-1 Supply or other manufacturers. Another problem with IGT's unit was that it required an AC outlet. Although most machines contain an AC outlet, when power was turned off to check the EPROM, it was necessary to use an extension cord to the nearest power outlet, often far away from the machine being tested.

Since IGT had no interest in marketing the comparator, this co-author developed several battery operated units to work on the various manufacturers' machines depending

on the type of EPROM being used. Also, when the bat-
teries were low in the comparator, it would indicate "no"
so that a bad memory chip would not inadvertently pass
the test. Crevelt Computer System, Inc. (CCS) sold many
of these units to the casinos and to the manufacturers who
in turn sold them to their machine customers.

When a casino suspects a jackpot is not legitimate or
refuses to pay due to a machine malfunction, the Gaming Control Board decides whether or not the player gets
paid. Slot players who have won big jackpots but are not
paid because of a Gaming Control Board decision can appeal their decision to a district court.

Malfunctioning Machines

Casinos must be very careful about arresting suspected
slot cheats. Dan Reaser, of the Nevada Gaming Division,
told attendees at a recent seminar about one case which
involved a player who discovered that a slot machine was
not working properly. By manipulating the handle a certain way he could get the first reel to line up cherries for
a win every time. Casino employees watched him for quite
awhile before calling the gaming authorities. The agents
also observed him for some time and then arrested him for
cheating. The prosecutor later dismissed the charges feeling it would be difficult to get a jury to agree that what
he was doing was really cheating or illegal. The man then
sued the casino for false arrest and won a judgment for
$25,000. The casino appealed and lost. The judge ruled
the casino to be negligent in not keeping the machine in
proper operating condition.

Another case recently involved a $5,000.00 jackpot

when a "little old lady" lined up three 7's on the pay line at a casino in Laughlin, Nevada. The board denied the jackpot, claiming a malfunction because one 7 was an eighth of an inch below the pay line. *An eighth of an inch!* She appealed. Clark County District Judge Thomas Foley ruled that she should be paid. The reason he gave, however, was that it would be bad public relations not to pay because Nevada depends so heavily on tourism. The case went to the State Supreme Court who upheld the district court ruling, also expressing concern for the state's image. The casino had to pay the $5,000.00 plus the attorney's fees.

SLOT PLAYERS, BEWARE! IF A MACHINE SEEMS TO DISPLAY THE SLIGHTEST IRREGULARITY DURING PLAY, LEAVE IT OR REPORT IT TO A CHANGE GIRL OR FLOORMAN FOR REPAIR. DON'T TAKE A CHANCE ON LOSING A JACKPOT OR HAVING TO GO TO COURT TO COLLECT YOUR WINNINGS.

All machines now have notices somewhere on them that "malfunction voids all plays." That means if you have a runaway machine (one that malfunctions and continues to pay more than it should) you will not be allowed to keep all that money. Our important rule bears repeating. If you hit a jackpot that doesn't pay off, and it is determined that the machine is not functioning properly (not necessarily because of cheating) you might not get paid. Therefore, we don't recommend that you continue to play a machine that is not working properly.

Incidentally, if a machine malfunctions by failing to register all the coins you have played, notify the change person and let a floorman check it for you. Generally, the casinos will reimburse you without question once or twice.

But if the machine continues to "steal" your coins, the floorman will probably shut it down until a mechanic checks it out.

Let's stay with the subject of malfunctioning machines because the problem seems to happen more frequently than expected, especially in the case of big jackpots. As we've just learned, the dispute between casino and player often ends up in court. Here's still another example.

Recently, a U.S. District Court in Philadelphia awarded 1.1 million dollars to a player after a dispute of two and a half years with an Atlantic City casino over a machine malfunction.

The player had to sue to collect the jackpot he hit on a video slot machine. The machine he was playing appeared to be malfunctioning before lights flashed and music blared and four winning symbols lined up on the screen. Then the symbols disappeared during an electrical malfunction.

The casino intends to petition for a new trial. If the notice about malfunctions voiding all play was properly posted, it could be interesting to see if the courts reverse their decision.

Another case of malfunction presented an interesting basis for litigation. In a downtown Las Vegas casino a man hit a progressive jackpot for $137,000.00. Unfortunately, the jackpot display had malfunctioned. It was supposed to read something like $1,187.00. The slot manager was livid. The jackpot had been read and recorded at the "correct" amount less than an hour before it was hit. The casino wanted to pay $1,187.00. The player is suing for $137,000.00. Interesting questions: *Does the progressive jackpot display for a bank of progressive machines constitute advertising and enticement to the player, who then invests money with a view toward an "advertised" possible gain? Or does a malfunction notice on individual machines also apply to the electronic display?* The real winners in this lawsuit may be the legal beagles with the most creative arguments.

Security

When you visit a major casino for the first time, note the large black "bubbles" hanging from the ceiling at various places. These bubbles contain video cameras that are focused on different areas to monitor slot machines, table games, change booths, etc. Behind the scene in a closed room, security personnel are employed around the clock to do nothing but watch the video screens to detect possible cheating.

John Stroup, slot manager of the Flamingo Hilton, demonstrated how he can zero in on any area covered by the camera from the monitor in his office. However, he cannot move the cameras himself. Only the director of security can do that for him. Otherwise, he might interrupt an important bit of surveillance at the wrong time.

Slot cheats apprehended have claimed that these cameras can be disabled by a special laser gun fired at them. Can the camera manufacturers develop a laser proof camera? Anything is possible if the need becomes urgent enough. Needless to say, improved methods of surveillance by casino security and beefed up law enforcement are needed to catch slot cheaters and to prosecute them.

Most of the losses are experienced by the state of Nevada. However, New Jersey has three times the manpower for law enforcement. Today, Nevada has 365 employees and seven prosecuting attorneys for the whole state. New Jersey employs three times the manpower and 29 prosecuting attorneys for only eleven casinos.

A good reason for this difference is that in New Jersey, gaming regulations require an agent to be in each casino during all operating hours. Casinos have to pick up the tab for gaming agents to be on duty in the casinos. Nevada does not have the same requirement. The combined budgets for the New Jersey Casino Control Commission and the Division of Gaming Enforcement total 41 million dollars or approximately two percent of the annual casino industry winnings.

Over a period of five years Nevada officials investigated 12,000 cases of cheating, but only 1,200 were referred for prosecution. No statistics are kept on the number of convictions.

Manufacturers have also had to increase security to prevent unauthorized access to their machine schematics and computer programs. One company learned the hard way when it was consolidating its Las Vegas and Reno operations. Employees from both areas were in and out of both facilities and no identification controls had been established.

One day a gentleman in a business suit walked in the back door and into the document control office. Without identifying himself, he asked for the drawings and schematics on their latest "XYZ" machine. He received the documents with no questions asked. He left by the back door, walked around the building and into the front door. There he identified himself as a gaming control agent and asked to see the chief engineer. Without a word, the agent handed the engineer the documents. The engineer's face turned red, white and probably blue in that order registering embarrassment, fear and anger. "Where did you get these?" he demanded. Not only did he learn how easily they were obtained but he received a severe lecture on the lack of security.

Any slot cheat in a business suit could have received those documents. That manufacturer (who will remain nameless to avoid embarrassment) quickly instituted one of the most stringent security and procedural control systems in the manufacturing industry.

The perils of acquiring the needed expertise for development of the sophisticated technology for today's burgeoning gaming industry are more numerous and dangerous than those of the legendary "Pauline." Finding someone with the knowledge and experience coupled with the business ethics to honor proprietary rights is not easy.

One manufacturer hired a university professor to program their "Race Horse" gaming device. The machine worked well, passed the Gaming Control Board's restrictions and trials and was reportedly making money for the casinos and the manufacturer. Then, for no apparent reason, the machine started losing money. The casino called the manufacturer who checked it out and could find no explanation for the change. The manufacturer decided to stake out the machine and observe the action to see what was going wrong. After several nights, the professor came in, played the machine awhile and was winning heavily. When confronted after several such wins, he admitted that he had found a "bug" in the program. He discovered a pattern at which the horse paying 100 to 1 would consistently recur. Instead of reporting it to the manufacturer, he was using the information to line his pockets with silver. The manufacturer quickly corrected the lack of random selection of winners in that program.

This professor's programming days for gaming projects are probably over. The manufacturer is also out of business and these machines have since been replaced by other manufacturers' models.

There is a constant "seesaw" with the casinos and manufacturers on one end developing "FOOL PROOF" electronics to protect the machines and the slot cheats on the other end literally going to school to learn about RAMS, ROMS, microprocessors, electronics and computer programming so they can "FOOL" the smart machines.

Can't you just see the curriculum? Scoff-Law 101, Basic Wiring 102, Creative Magnetics 104, Beat-the-Clock 123, Laser-Camera Interface, and Black Box Building for Successful Cheating. If you flunk practical experience by getting caught, take post graduate work in Finger Pointing and Plea Bargaining for Self Preservation. But don't forget your doctorate in Establishing a New Identity!

Seriously though, the Nevada legislature has enacted regulations for stiff penalties for those convicted of cheating. You could be sentenced for five to 20 years in prison and fined from $25,000 to triple the amount of your cheating gains. Cheaters can also be required to forfeit anything used in cheating operations, including homes, cars, boats, mechanical devices, etc.

So, if you have any idea of trying to cheat the machines, forget it. As John Gollehon advises in his book *All About Slots and Video Poker*, three things you leave at home are "slugs, washers, and your Black & Decker drill." After all "losing a few dollars beats losing a few years."

CHAPTER 9

Regulatory Safeguards

"All gambling is crooked."

"All gambling machines and games are rigged."

"You can't win the big jackpot."

"If anyone wins a big jackpot, he's probably a front for the casino or the crooks who run them."

Have you heard these or similiar remarks? We have. They're prevalent throughout non-gaming states. Perhaps, you have wondered if they are true. How honest are the casinos? Are all slot machines rigged? A brief explanation of the regulatory safeguards designed to protect the public may reassure you somewhat.

Federal controls are minimal. The federal government

prohibits gambling on federal military bases within the United States. However, it allows gaming in its installations overseas. **The legalization, regulation and control of gaming activities are reserved for the states.** Exceptions are interstate transportation and transmission over public communication lines which are still controlled by federal agencies. Another exception is gaming on Indian reservations which is unique in that they are subject only to federal restrictions and not to most of their state and local agencies. The status of Indian gaming is currently a quagmire of conflicting federal, state and Indian rights and jurisdictions. It can only be clarified by congressional action, which traditionally makes matters worse.

Transporting The Machines

Licenses to manufacture, operate and distribute slot machines do not grant immunity from federal laws against transporting of gaming devices across state lines or into states where gambling is prohibited. Manufacturers are subject to surveillance not only by state authorities but also by federal investigators.

The federal government has strict guidelines for the interstate transportation of gaming devices and paraphernalia. Transportation is only allowed between states where the manufacture and/or use of such devices is allowed.

One morning this co-author walked into a manufacturer's office and found the place crawling with FBI agents. Employees were being "grilled" individually for information on a certain person and his connection, if any, with the manufacturer. It seems that person was suspected of transporting slots from the Las Vegas area into the New

York City area, where they are obviously illegal. Neither the manufacturer nor any of its employees had any business dealings with the suspect. They were dumbfounded when shortly after the FBI agents left, the suspect walked in the door! Needless to say, no one offered to buy him lunch.

More recently, indictments were handed down on 22 suspected members of a ring of slot "transporters" who lived in Las Vegas, Texas, California and on the East Coast. It was estimated that they had bought thousands of machines in Las Vegas and shipped them to various illegal gaming spots in the east.

Gaming machines that are modified to serve as "amusement only" devices are shipped all over the country and are found in bars, private clubs and homes. The possibility that many are used for gambling doesn't take much stretching of the imagination.

However, machines manufactured before 1948 are considered antiques in most states and are legal as collector's items and for home use. The guidelines for transporting these antiques must still be followed, which may include inspection by state authorities at the sending and receiving locations.

Here's more on the subject of owning antique slots, as excerpted from *Las Vegas Behind the Tables PART 2,* Barney Vinson's sequel to his original bestseller:

"Most states allow a person the right to own a slot machine *if* it is to be used for collecting purposes only, and *if* it will not be used for gambling. In order for the machine to be a collector's item, it usually has to be 25 years old . . . which rules out electronic slots for private owners.

"The ages vary from one state to the next, and most state laws are fairly simple. For instance, Missouri says 'any machine over 30 years old is presumed to be an antique.' New York: 'Any machine manufactured prior to 1950 is presumed to be an antique.' In Arizona 'any machine manufactured 25 years ago is presumed to be an antique.' But then in Virginia 'present laws are unclear.' In Texas, watch out! 'When a slot machine is purchased by a state citizen it is required that within 30 days of purchase the buyer supplies name of machine, year of manufacture, and serial number to local law enforcement agency. Failure to do so is constituted as a *felony*.' In other words, if the machine is 30, and you do not report it within 30, then *you* do 30.''

Vinson also wrote about the grading of machines based on their condition. In his own witty style, Vinson said:

''Once an individual decides to buy a slot machine, it is a good idea to grab hold of something like the Loose Change Blue Book, which lists the prices of various machines, from Grade 1 (top of the line) to Grade 5. (How'd you get it over here, Chuck, on the back of your skateboard?)''

Operating The Machine

In Nevada, the Gaming Commission and Gaming Control Board are the regulatory bodies responsible for licensing and regulating of all gaming activites. The corresponding body in New Jersey is the Alantic City Casino Control Commission.

According to the Regulations of the Nevada Gaming Commission and State Gaming Control Board there are two major classifications of licenses issued, Restricted and Non-Restricted.

A "restricted license permits the operation of slot machines only in an establishment wherein the operation of the machines is incidental to the primary business of the licensee." Fifteen (15) machines is the maximum allowed at one location.

Non-gaming establishments permit an operator to place machines as an added attraction for customers. They may receive a percentage of the profit from the machines or a straight fee, depending upon their agreement with the operator. However, they must be "acceptable" to the gaming regulators before an operator is permitted to place machines in their establishment. For instance, a legitimate business (restaurant, pizza parlor, supermarket, etc.) operated by a suspected underworld figure or former casino employee ousted for illegal activities would not be "acceptable" for placement of gaming machines.

Casinos and casino-hotels must obtain "non-restricted" licenses. Owners and key employees must pass the "acid" test. Applicants must undergo extensive background investigations. Further, the applicant must pay all expenses related to the background investigation which could vary from a few thousand to several *hundred* thousand dollars.

When the Gaming Board approved an increase in the number of machines for restricted licensees from 15 to 25 recently, a special meeting of the board was called during which all the "big guns" from the major casinos in Nevada and the Nevada Resort Association objected to the increase. They convinced the Board that it would be faced with enforcement and control problems.

After hearing arguments from both the "little guys" and the "giants," the Board took a second vote. It was decided the slot limit for the small businesses shall remain at

15. In the "Super Bowl of Slots," the giants always win.

Incidentally, you do not need a license to purchase a slot machine for private use in your own "game room" for entertainment, provided your state allows it. But don't allow friends to play with their own money, don't retain their losses, and don't pay them for jackpots won. You could be accused of illegal gaming. You might even alienate your friends if they play for fun and then change their minds and want to be paid when they hit a jackpot!

Designing the Machine

The procedures that manufacturers must follow to obtain a license for a new gaming device are strict, time consuming, and expensive. They not only have to spend big bucks for research and development of new devices, but also must design it with a view toward the factors that the Gaming Control Board will use to examine the new product. A brief tour through the procedure will give you some idea of how and why some machines have been around for years and some disappear within a few months.

The Gaming Control Board's main concerns in approving new gaming devices are that they are reliable, fair to the player, and have player appeal to generate a profit for the casino and the resulting tax revenue.

Steps in obtaining approval to manufacture and market a new machine are briefly described as follows:

1. Manufacturer produces a working prototype.

2. Manufacturer submits it to the Board along with the source code for its computer program.

3. The Board laboratory examines it thoroughly, plays

it, hits it with hammers, tries to cheat it, and abuses it every way possible.

4. Two or three technicians or computer "experts" look at the source code and write an opinion on whether or not it works and will be profitable for the casino.

5. If it is recommended, it will be put on the agenda for a public meeting of the Board and approval given for a field trial.

6. Manufacturer must then find a casino willing to put it on the floor and document the results for a 60 to 90 day period.

7. The machine and the record of activity then go back to the Board and it is put on the agenda for the next meeting.

8. The Board studies the record of activity during the trial period including data on amount of play, how well it worked or didn't work, and how much money it made for the casino.

9. The Board then decides whether or not to grant a license for its manufacture and distribution. Sometimes they will grant a conditional license provided certain modifications are made.

Gaming Board meetings sometimes become very lively, especially when controversial figures or celebrities appear for hearings or licensing. Small manufacturers who do not employ full time attorneys usually retain lawyers to represent them at such hearings. Some of these "part-time" counselors took umbrage when at one meeting a board member referred to the various legal beagles present as "in-house and out-house counselors."

While working as a consultant with one company to examine their new machine and to help get it into shape for approval by the Gaming Control Board, we discovered a routine in the program that guaranteed the machine would hold its percentage. For instance, if the machine paid out 96 percent and was supposed to be paying 92 percent, the routine would throw out any winners until its percentage got back on line! A revolting development!

We cautioned them that such a routine was against the law and would have to be removed before it would ever get by the Board. We can only assume that the final version that was approved by the Board, and is now on the street, had that illegal routine removed. But your guess is as good as ours.

One machine that had a rough time getting Board approval was the "Whirl Win" developed by IGT. The Board objected to its similarity to the old carnival pusher-type games that were often rigged. The machine displayed coins that appeared ready to drop from a shelf into a payout chute, but which seldom ever dropped. IGT finally got it approved and it has done quite well. In its infancy, however, it usually paid out more than it was supposed to and had to be modified with extra baffles to hold its percentage.

At one time, Harrah's hotel and casino in Reno had their own Research and Development department and were designing their own slot machine. They also built a contraption they dubbed "The Iron Grandma" which would literally play and test the machines. It would insert coins and pull the handle. But Harrah's was not satisfied with their own machine design and hired a nationwide consulting firm to design a machine for them. The firm developed a beautiful machine, with a multiple-board system, an optical reel-reading system, and a very elaborate mechanical handle. However, the handle was too delicate for the rigorous play of Iron Grandma. Grandma ripped the handle off after a few pulls. Also, if the handle was greased too lightly or too heavily, it would break easier. The designer didn't believe that players were as abusive as the Grandma and apparently not aware of the noise, smoke, static, and dirty environment found in most casinos. The fifteen machines they built were placed in the casino and taken out almost immediately. They were easily shocked by the static and would literally display "garbage." The bar-coding on the back of the reels would get smudged and dirty, "blinding" the optical reader so that it would either fail to read, mis-read, or cause the machine to mis-pay. Needless to say, the machine was never approved.

The Nevada Gaming Board acquired one of Harrah's Iron Grandmas to test new machines submitted for approval. Unfortunately, they underestimated Gramdma's strength. The first machine they tested was not bolted down and Grandma literally threw it across the room on the first handle pull.

Iron Grandma reminds us of the story told us by a change girl about one of her steady customers. The little white-haired grandmotherly woman always talked to her machine in a sweet soft voice and caressed it before pulling the handle. One day she overheard "Granny" say as she patted the machine gently on the side, "Now you pay me, you sweet thing, and I'll be nice to you." About an hour and approximately $60 later she paused to hear Granny say in the same soft tone, "You'd better pay me you S.O.B. or I'm gonna kick you in the face and break your arm!"

Probably the best way of testing machines is to have them played by "trained gorillas." Jennings, a slot manufacturer, furnished machines to Army bases overseas and were proud of their strong handle design. One day they got a call from an overseas base complaining that an irate player from a construction battalion went into a rage when he lost and ripped the handle out of the machine. Jennings engineers couldn't believe a man could be strong enough to do that until they received the mangled handle and machine.

How well a machine will stand up under normal playing conditions is one factor that the Board considers before granting approval. You wouldn't believe the abuse that the machines get from players and would-be cheaters. We once saw an irate loser slap the logo glass so hard it broke. The change girl alerted the floorman to shut the machine down immediately before some possible cheater could try to empty it. Spilling drinks, kicking, and jamming of knives, keys, nail files and other objects into the coin slot to release a stuck coin are some of the ways players cause a machine to malfunction.

A Major Problem — Gambling Addiction

Although this book describes the excitement, the thrill, and the glamour surrounding slot machines, we would be remiss if we did not include a strong caution against the possibility of becoming addicted to those fascinating devices.

As we indicated at the beginning of this chapter, regulatory safeguards are designed to make sure machines work properly and to protect the public from dishonest casinos. But how do you protect the people from themselves? Quite obviously, neither a Gaming Control Board agent nor a casino boss is going to step in when you've spent too much money and tell you to "hit the door." Needless to say, there are far too many players who could certainly use that kind of "mothering." Far too many players who simply go too far.

Sue Miller, in the Baltimore Evening Sun, reported that a conservative national estimate of compulsive gamblers is four to six million, with 35 percent of them being women. A pioneer in the treatment of pathological gamblers is Taylor Manor Hospital in Ellicott City, Maryland. They predict that by the turn of the century 50 percent of them will probably be women.

In addition to possible family heartaches and financial difficulties, another dangerous result of gambling addiction is about $2 billion a year in thefts and embezzlements to support the habit.

Resorts International in Atlantic City posted the telephone number of New Jersey's hot line for compulsive gamblers in seven places, at the entrances and over the cashier cages. The signs also bear the slogan "Bet With Your Head, Not Over It." The toll-free number, 1-800-GAMBLER, reaches New Jersey's Council on Compulsive Gambling, a non-profit organization dedicated to counseling addicted gamblers.

In Las Vegas there are 21 different meetings of Gamblers Anonymous. There is Gamanon for families and friends of compulsive gamblers, GAM-A-TEEN for children of addicted parents, and Gamblers Victorious which tries to convince sufferers that they can be cured of their addictions.

According to Miller, a symposium sponsored by the Ellicott City hospital drew 365 psychologists, psychiatrists, therapists, and counselors. Joanne Franklin, director of training in the treatment program at the hospital, said that gambling addiction is very often associated with drug and alcohol addiction. Compulsive gambling also afflicts men in their early adolescent years but does not generally afflict women until their 30's or 40's. Female gamblers are usually more depressed than male gamblers but the suicide attempt rate with male gamblers is 20 percent higher than from other problems.

Although there are no "regulatory" safeguards against gambling addiction, it appears that the states and cities are aware of the problem and are supportive of groups concerned about and attempting to deal with the issue.

A Minor Problem

The legal age for gambling is 21. Anyone under that age is allowed in the restaurants, gift shops, and video arcades. They may walk through the casinos enroute to such areas but they cannot play or loiter in the gaming areas.

The minor problem is a major one in Atlantic City. According to New Jersey's Division of Gaming Enforcement, 34,387 juveniles were caught on casino floors in 1986. One seventeen year old was wined and dined by casinos while she gambled away thousands of dollars. She was fined $500 and received a suspended sentence after pleading guilty. Her probation was conditioned on her attending Gamblers Anonymous.

The "Kick Yourself in the Rear" award must go to the family from Arkansas who were playing slots at Caesars Palace in Las Vegas. The "Million Dollar Baby" jackpot carousel was hit for $1,061,811 by the 19-year-old son. His parents were playing nearby. Realizing he could not collect the jackpot, the 225 pound, 6 foot 5 inch player left the machine and alerted his father to claim it. However, the surveillance cameras recorded the underage player at the machine when it hit, even though his parents had been playing it earlier. The Gaming Control Board ordered Caesars not to pay and not to divulge the name of the player and his family.

The family retained a Las Vegas lawyer to sue for the jackpot. Part of the argument may be that two teenage sisters were also playing slots unchallenged by casino personnel. It is understandable that they could easily have overlooked the son as a minor because of his size, but the casino is obligated to check the ID of obvious minors, not only playing machines but just standing and watching which is also prohibited.

Unfortunately, with so many people playing, casino employees can't constantly be checking ID's; they're too busy. However, they do the best job they can and we have seen them check many players who look underage.

The moral of this story is obvious. Don't gamble if you're under 21.

Perhaps this information has assured you that gaming and slot playing does not completely fit the derogatory image as portrayed in the movies and television specials. These safeguards have virtually eliminated the overt criminal elements. It is a legal form of recreation which can be enjoyed *with moderation* and with virtual certainty of an "honest" game.

CHAPTER 10

Slot Machine
Promotions

Casinos have learned to "go with the flow" or, more appropriately, "go with the dough." The trend toward increased revenue from slot machines over that received from all other games combined is like the proverbial hole in the dike or the yeast that makes the bread rise.

As casinos add more slot machines to accommodate the players, they also devise more ways to attract the players to their carousels. What a Merry-Go-Round it becomes as everyone tries to catch the brass ring, or the silver and gold ring in this case!

Slot Tournaments

One of the "lures" to attract these visitors is slot tournaments.

Tournaments for slot players grow more popular and widespread each year, while the prizes for winning increase with the number of participants.

"Slots Hysteria," the second tournament held by the Flamingo Hilton in Las Vegas, featured a prize fund of $100,000. Entry fee was $550 and included hotel room, welcome gift, meals and an awards dinner dance. Tournament machines were selected by random drawing prior to each session and winnings accumulated on a meter. Partners could play, but only one at a time.

"Slot's Hysteria II" at the Flamingo followed with a prize fund of $270,000 based on 600 entries. Entry fee was $777 and first place was $50,000.

The Sands holds slot tournaments approximately every five weeks, each with a different theme. An "Oldie but Goodie" '50s/'60s theme tournament with a $325,000 stake was a good example. Another tournament theme was "Life of the Rich and Famous."

The Aladdin Hotel's slot tournament, with only a $200 entry fee, offered prizes of $30,000 for first place, $15,000 for second, $10,000 for third, $4,000 for fourth and $1,000 each for fifth through twentieth place. Entrants played three 45-minute sessions on three different types of machines. The top eight scorers on each type of machine advanced into the semi-final round and the top four competed in the "Final Four Pull Off."

The Golden Nugget holds its "Grand Prix of Slots Tournament" with a $100,000 Grand prize. $2,400 entry fee covers the usual accommodations, awards dinner, etc. All of the entry money is returned in 36 prizes totaling $360,000 for the three-day tournament.

The Flamingo Hilton held annual tournaments of champions for their winners of the $250,000 Pot O' Gold progressive jackpots. Tournament winners got one million dollars!

When we interviewed John Stroup, slot manager at the Flamingo Hilton, he stated that these annual million dollar tournaments had been discontinued. Their Pot-O-Gold progresssive jackpots were also frozen at $250,000. Their reasoning was that a quarter of a million dollars is attractive enough for the tourists who account for the largest portion of their clientele. As Mr. Stroup put it, "The Hilton hotels were the pioneers of the six figure jackpots. Then all the casinos started playing the one-upsmanship game with million dollar and multi-million dollar jackpots. Such large winners are now so common that they get only small coverage in the news media, and the lotteries are awarding such big jackpots that even those wins are getting minor mention." Mr. Stroup also said that with smaller jackpots, they can afford to "loosen" the machines, lower the house percentage, and provide more frequent payouts. "After all, a guest who comes to town for four days and loses all his money the first day trying to hit a million dollars and then has to sit around broke the rest of the time leaves with a bad taste in his mouth and a negative impresssion of the city." Unhappy guests don't often return.

However, since that interview the Flamingo and Hilton hotels have installed $1,000,000 progressive jackpots, to compete with the Barbary Coast next door and Caesars Palace across the street.

At the Fremont, a Boyd group hotel in downtown Las

Vegas, a slot tournament runs Sunday through Thursday with only a $10.00 buy-in for each round. After five rounds (held hourly), two final rounds are held. Besides cash prizes, first through third places receive a free entry into the Super Slot Payoff and a complimentary entry for tournament night held every fifth week. Top Super Prize is $25,000. With the low entry fee, the Boyd hotels really know how to hold a slot tournament! But, of course, they can afford it. In addition to Sam's Town on Boulder Highway, they also own the Stardust, the California, and Sam's Town Gold River in Laughlin, Nevada, on the Colorado River bordering Arizona.

Caesars Palace invited slot players to "Loot the Roman Empire" with its $450,000 Olympic Tournament. After four days of play, winners received $100,000 for first place, $50,000 for second and $20,000 for third. Entry fee was $2,000, which also included the usual accommodations, gifts and a Hawaiian luau awards banquet with prizes awarded by the world-famous comedian, Red Skelton. According to their ad, "All can be yours, with just a little pull."

The Riviera Hotel hosted its third "Pull For the Gold" tournament with $200,000 in prize money. First prize for the tournament was $50,000. Top prize for the winner of each round was $2,000. Entry fee was $1,000, which included accommodations for four days and three nights, meals, welcome gifts, party awards banquet, and free Riviera show for two. Prizes were paid down to 125th place.

These tournaments have been so successful that even before the April tournament was over, the Riviera announced the next "Pull for Gold" to be held only three months later! First prize was $250,000!

The tournament attracted 388 players and awarded

more than $650,000. Do you consider yourself a born loser? Consider this! The guy who came in last with the lowest number of points drove away in a brand new Lincoln Town Car! They can hand me a booby prize like that anytime!

Automobiles, trips, and houses offered for last prize make the tournament more interesting and competitive. Players often deliberately try to be last because they think it is easier to win a nice prize that way than to lose out on the super first prize.

These prizes are not "small potatoes." The Riviera has learned which side of the bread the butter is on or maybe we should say they have learned who to "butter up" to bring in the "bread." A more recent tournament was for $1,600,000 in prizes with first place of $1,000,000 and prizes paid through 550 places. There were 48 first and second place session winners of $2,000 and $1,000 each respectively. Last place prize was a week's vacation for two in Hawaii. Also, the entry fee for this tournament was lowered from $2500 to $1750.

Why are slot tournaments so popular? Of course, the prizes are the main incentive. But there seems to be a "competitive spirit" in man that urges him to pit his resources and his skills against other people, against forces of nature, and even against insurmountable odds. This same "spirit" urges a young boy to challenge his friend in a race, and nations to send their athletes to the Olympic Games. Perhaps it also accounts for a slot player's preference for the progressive banks of machines. He is competing against *other* players as well as the machine.

The most important reason for the player may be that in the slot tournament there are guaranteed prizes at the end for lucky participants. The odds of winning a prize of some kind are more realistic.

The bottom line on slot tournaments *for the casino* is their ability to "capture" slot players. Tournaments last from two or three days to a week for "out-of-towners."

What do you think those slot players do when they are not playing their tournament session? Practicing, that's what! Practicing on the casino's other slot machines. Their entry fee is paid in advance, and you can bet that if they put up a few hundred or even a few thousand for an entry fee, they bring a lot more for "practice."

The Million Dollar Money Machine Bust

One slot promotion in Atlantic City turned sour for the casino, even though it was popular for the participants. Several years ago, the Atlantic City Sands Hotel and Casino announced a million dollar prize game. Free tickets were published in newspapers and handed out in the casino. The ticket contained a set of symbols which could be matched to those displayed on a slot-like machine in the casino to win one million dollars. The million dollars had to be claimed within 15 minutes after the winning symbols were displayed, otherwise the prize was only one hundred dollars. There were strict rules, one which prohibited playing with more than one card per person. The reels were spun six times daily — six potential one million dollar winners!

The promotion began the day after Labor Day and was supposed to continue through January of the following year (about four months).

Michael Sherry, a member of the New York Futures Exchange, learned of the promotion about the middle of September and started studying the game. He made daily trips to Atlantic City to watch the spin for two weeks before he matched the symbols and won the million. A few days later he predicted that the promotion would be cancelled before January because it was too easy to win.

Sure enough, less than one month later Joseph Ryan matched for another million. He had quit his job as a window washer and watched every spin for six weeks before scoring.

Sherry had not yet received any payment when Ryan won. Payments were supposed to be $50,000 per year for 20 years.

Within hours after Ryan's win, the casino placed an "out of order" sign on the machine and cancelled the promotion. It was obvious someone had figured this one out.

Five people filed a class action suit charging consumer fraud, claiming damages, and demanding that the game be reinstated. The judge ruled that by advertising the casino had entered into a contract with the public. He did not rule that there had been fraud, leaving that for those filing suit for damages to prove. He ruled also that the casino did not have to reinstate the game. Litigants who could prove that they lost money for travel expenses to play the game and did not know that it had been cancelled could be reimbursed for those expenses plus attorney's fees.

The County Division of Consumer Affairs investigated the possibility of false advertising. The casino could have been penalized $2,000 for consumer fraud on a first offense. Big deal! They probably saved another two or three million dollars or more by cancelling. It would take thousands of litigants for a few hundred dollars damages each to add up to the millions they saved.

Other Slot Promotions

One of the strangest promotions has to be this one, put on by Harrah's Marina in Atlantic City. They offered $20 in credit that could be used in any of their restaurants to anyone who could produce an income tax return showing they reported a jackpot over $1,200. (Jackpots over $1,200 are automatically reported to the IRS by the casino; those under that amount are the responsibility of the player to report.)

Had Harrah's designed their promotion for reported jackpots *under* $1,200, we doubt that there would have been many takers!

In Atlantic City, the Division of Gaming Enforcement (DGE) ordered two casinos to stop publishing "deceptive and misleading" slot machine advertisements:

Trump's Castle advertised:

"Slot players lost $18 million more playing at Harrah's than at Trump."

Harrah's ad:

"Harrah's slot players won $79 million more than the Castle. Where are you playing?"

The Division considered these ads misleading because they didn't indicate the number or denomination of the slot machines.

In Las Vegas, the Continental Hotel-Casino's "Golden Opportunity" promotion featured prizes of $5, $20, $50, and $100 cash, dinners for two, free buffets, T-shirts, satin jackets, golf shirts, caps and tote bags. Players won these prizes by cashing in special "gold" coins received in payouts from the machines. All slot, video poker and keno machines were peppered with the special coins.

At the Palace Station, a special promotion included registering for one free ticket per day to win weekly prizes of $100, $500 and a Cadillac. Additional tickets for the drawing were given for every $25 jackpot hit on the slots. This promotion is alternated with an annual "Car-A-Day in May" drawing. That's 31 automobiles to be won by lucky players during the month. Many players complain that receiving drawing tickets only for jackpots won was unfair. They felt that tickets should be given for change purchased because they often invested hundreds of dollars to "win" one or two tickets. However, the casinos don't "trust" players to play all the money they buy.

The Lady Luck in downtown Las Vegas installed a bank of "Can't Lose" machines to introduce their new 16-story "Luxury Tower." You either win on the machines (maximum payout is $1,000), or you get the money you invested back. Lady Luck has these machines set at 120 to 130 percent return to the customers. In the first few months of testing, 59 players hit $1,000 jackpots and the casino says thousands hit smaller payouts. Out-of-state customers with their "Fun Books" get a free pull on the special machines. Also, four times a day winners in a drawing get to play two minutes each. Don't expect to be able to play these machines as long or as often as you like. They're merely another lure to get you a "warm" feeling that all their machines are generous.

When you come to town, check around, it seems like

there's a new promotion going on all the time at one hotel or another.

Our friend, Barney Vinson, who wrote *Las Vegas Behind The Tables PART 2* at about the same time we were writing *our* book, included some amusing stories about slot machine promotions in his sequel. Here are two particular stories that caught our fancy:

"In one casino, a slot machine boss came up with a meloncholy idea. 'I was driving down the Strip,' one oldtimer recalled, 'and I see this old fella walking down the side of the road carrying a watermelon. Then a couple of blocks later I see another fella carrying a watermelon. I'm wondering what the hell's going on, and then I see someone coming out of this casino carrying a watermelon. I went inside, and there was a watermelon on top of every single slot machine in the joint — and a sign which said, 'With every watermelon jackpot, win a big prize!'

"Another slot manager offered free personalized key chains just for coming inside. Of course, he just happened to be out of key chains with your name on them, 'but we'll have one made up right away,' In the meantime, two slot machines set up on either side of the key chain booth were spitting out jackpots right and left. Since there were some empty machines nearby, and since the key chain would be ready any minute now — 'Oh, what the heck, give me ten dollars in nickels.'

'Hey, that's a nice key chain, Boob.'

'That's supposed to say 'Bob.' And the damn thing cost me SEVENTY-FIVE DOLLARS!!' "

Our thanks to Barney for allowing us to use his stories.

Free Pull Slots

Circus Circus has an ongoing promotion with free pulls

on special slot machines. You receive coupons for the free pulls when you ride the shuttle from the Manor or Skyrise to the main casino, or as you leave the buffet. The free-pull machines are located in strategic spots in the main, west, Skyrise and Manor casinos. They are all near a change booth, so if you win, even if it is only a key chain, you might be tempted to try your luck on the "real" machines.

Bally's in Las Vegas held its own unique version of a "Free Pull" contest, only requiring registration for a drawing. Each daily winner drawn then got a free pull on every slot machine (except video poker) in the hotel, *all 890 of them!* Each day's play took approximately two and one-half hours with a potential of winning $2.7 million. There were no "really big" winners; however, each winner averaged $800 to $1,000. Not bad for a *zero* investment.

Recently, the Reno Hilton staged its "Don't be a Sucker" campaign. Free Dum-Dum suckers were handed out with wrappers for a free pull on the "Top Slot," a $1 machine with a new car as a prize. Somehow this promotion suggests a contradiction in its title, luring all the "suckers" into the casino to play the regular slots when they don't win on the free pull.

One of the most popular promotions had to be the "MONEY FOR NOTHIN" giveaway held by Harrah's Tahoe. While enjoying a nice dinner or playing your favorite game, a special "Money for Nothin" showgirl may have walked up and handed you cash, anywhere from $100 to $3,000. It happened every half hour between 11:00 a.m. and 3:00 a.m., seven days a week. No drawings, no tickets, no registrations; you just had to be there.

Advertised Percentages

Recently, the Reno Hilton placed gold-plated signs on each machine indicating the programmed percentage of payout. For instance: "This machine is verified by the manufacturer to return 97.84 percent." The percentages differ from machine to machine and range from 97 to 99 percent. The promotion was so successful in Reno that the signs were also posted on machines at the Las Vegas Hilton. Of the 1,004 slots and videos, 104 special machines were posted: 67 were $1.00, 31 were $5.00 and 6 were $25.00 machines. Cecil Fredi, slot manager, said they took a survey and found that the players didn't play a machine posted 99 percent any more frequently than one posted 97 percent!

All the posted machines are three-reelers with medium-size jackpots. A $1 machine pays $1,199 for three jokers. A $5 machine pays as high as $6,000 for three "crazy bars," and the $25 machine pays $25,000 for three 7-bars. Although the Las Vegas & Flamingo Hiltons are noted for their huge Pot O'Gold jackpots, Fredi said, "I'd rather see 1,000 people win $1,000 jackpots than to see one person win $200,000."

Slot Manager Brian Bulmer of the Imperial Palace in Las Vegas announced recently that their machines pay 92 percent overall regardless of machine denomination. Of the Imperial's 968 slot machines, 164 are nickel, 485 are quarter, 10 are half dollar, 305 are dollar and 4 are five dollar machines. Sixty to seventy of the dollar slots are the popular "Magnificent 7" which have twelve combinations to pay $1,000 jackpots. Echoing Fredi at the Hilton, Bulmer stated, "I would rather give 60 people $1,000 than one person $60,000."

What these managers really mean is that more people winning means more people returning to their casino to try their luck again. The casinos derive more revenue from sixty or a thousand happy players than from two or three winners who return and thousands of losers who don't.

Bonus Credit and Player Tracking

An innovative concept of using a credit-card system was devised by Electronic Data Technology (EDT) a subsidiary of IGT. The machines include a slot for insertion of the credit card which accumulates bonus points for coins played. The player registers and receives the free credit card, or multiple cards to play more than one machine. Points are accumulated in the casino's special computer with each visit and machine played. Bonus points can be used toward prizes or cash. Rules vary with each casino. When you insert the credit card in the special slot attached to the machine, an electronic display greets you. For instance: "Hello, Joe, you have 37 bonus points. Coins to next bonus point: 40." Machines with different denominations require a different number of coins to be played for each bonus point (e.g. 28 on dollar machines, 110 on quarter machines.) Coins played without the credit card inserted do not decrease the count required for the bonus. But you can look for machines where the count has been lowered by other players who quit or ran out of money before reaching the bonus "countdown."

At the Sands, for example, points can be used to apply toward purchases in the gift shop, toward hotel room charges, meals, etc.

At Harrah's, points are accumulated continuously with

gifts awarded at various point levels. The grand prize from Harrah's is an antique slot machine.

At the Gold Coast, points can be used towards merchandise or hotel services. However, at the Gold Coast, points are earned for coins won, rather than coins played.

The Five Star Slot Club at Sam Boyd's Fremont attracted many members with its bonus points based on "coins in" rather than coins won. A 35-mm camera can be "bought" for 3,000 points and a 13-inch color TV for 11,725 points. All 1,039 machines including poker, keno and reel slots can be played for bonus points.

You can join the "24 Karat Club" at the Golden Nugget, Las Vegas, and receive bonus tickets while playing the specially marked dollar and five-dollar slots. Tickets can be accumulated for certificates good for cash rebates in gaming tokens, goods or services.

Bally's Park Place, Atlantic City, won honorable mention from "Gaming & Wagering Business" in their annual awards for best slot promotion. Bally's pink and purple MVP (most valuable player) tracking card was hyped with a tag line, "Bet with your head, not over it." That's good advice no matter who offers it.

These "credit card" systems have a dual role in the casinos. They are designed to attract players with the "bonus" feature. But they function primarily as "player tracking systems." The data fed into the central computer from each card allows the casino to determine who the slot "high rollers" are, the amount and frequency of play, which machines are most popular, how often and for what reason machines malfunction, total revenue and payout per machine, frequency of jackpots, percentage of profit for the casino, etc.

The bonuses offered to the players are to ensure more

rapid player acceptance and participation and thereby provide more accurate accounting and player tracking. Casinos may then be able to identify their best customers and reward them with more incentives to return and play.

Veteran slot players, however, have not fully grasped the concept of credit-card play. For instance, players keep walking away from the machine and leaving the cards in the slots. Other players or casino personnel find them and turn them in at the cage or "club" desk. At the Gold Coast we observed players retrieving these "lost" cards. "That's just today's stack," remarked the employee searching through a box of approximately 100 cards.

You also have to insert the card correctly to get bonus credit. One lady inserted the card backwards and didn't bother to read the display, "Insertion Error." She played for about half an hour before another player pointed out her mistake.

CHAPTER 11

Superstitions

Superstition, the belief in a supernatural force that can change or predict a course of events, is a part of all of our daily lives in one way or another, whether we are conscious of it or not. How often have you "crossed your fingers" to hope you get the job before or after an interview? When we fail in an attempt to do a difficult task, we might say, "It just wasn't in the cards."

People who claim not to be superstitious repeat superstitious customs every day. Did you ever wish upon a star or make a wish before blowing out the candles on your birthday cake? Did you ever break a chicken's wishbone with someone to see which of your wishes would come true?

Have you thrown a penny into a wishing well or into Trevi Fountain in Rome to make sure you return again? Did anyone throw rice at your wedding? That belief stems from an ancient custom to assure that the union would prove to be a fruitful one with many children.

How many of you avoid walking under a ladder or opening an umbrella in the house? Ever scratch your nose when it itched and said, "Company's coming"? And, of course, if you accidentally put your underwear, your pajamas, or your socks on wrong side out, you don't dare change them; that's bad luck!

If your left palm itches, you will be receiving money from an unlikely source, but you must scratch it on wood to make it good. If your right palm itches, you're going to shake hands with a stranger. If the bottom of your foot itches, you're going to take a trip or walk on new ground. Have you ever escaped a minor or major catastrophe and knocked on wood to make sure your good luck continued?

Gamblers may be more superstitious than anyone. And their beliefs or methods of influencing "Lady Luck" are as varied as the fish in the sea. Let's categorize some of them.

Charms, Amulets, and Fetishes

You all know that a rabbit's foot is lucky (except for the rabbit). And any horseshoe is lucky as long as you hang it properly on the wall, that is, with the open end up so your luck won't run out, or with the open end down, so the luck will pour out to you. We've heard both versions.

One slot player gets angry when someone sets a coin cup upside down on top of his machine when he's playing. He sets it right side up before inserting another coin. Another player insists the cup must be upside down on top of the machine, so the luck or "phantom" coins will somehow pour out of it through the machine and into his tray.

Finding a four-leaf clover is a sign of impending good fortune. Also, "See a penny, pick it up; all the day you'll have good luck. See a penny, let it lay; bad luck will follow you all day." Remember the penny loafers? It was bad luck to wear them without putting a lucky penny in the special slot on top, preferably a coin minted in the year of your birth.

One slot player carries a keychain with a small silver horseshoe. Imbedded in plastic inside the horseshoe are his lucky penny on one side and a four leaf clover on the other side. How can this guy possibly lose?

The Fitzgerald Casino/Hotel in Las Vegas stresses this lucky motif to its utmost. Their "Luck of the Irish" theme is carried out in carpets with four-leaf clovers and a "Lucky Forest" exhibit described as "an adult petting zoo to help gamblers become luckier." There is a water-filled wishing well complete with Blarney stones and an "imprisoned leprechaun" echo. There is a display of 15,000 genuine four-leaf clovers. Employees wear leprechaun uniforms. A special "Blarney Castle" slot area features genuine stones from the legendary Irish Castle. If you're an O'Mally, O'Reilly or even an O'Schultz or O'Smith, how can you be unlucky in such surroundings.

Remember when St. Christopher medals were worn to ward off danger? Now we hear that St. Christopher is out. Seems that after re-examination, his "miracles" fell short of the required qualifications and he was stripped of his "sainthood."

Barney Vinson in *Las Vegas Behind the Tables* tells of

the lady who played frequently at the Dunes, always bringing her lucky *Rosary Beads*, "each bead a small dice complete with little numbers on it."

In Lottery & Gaming Review, a full page advertisement offered a 24 karat gold plated Cross of Fatima which also contained a bit of the Hallowed Earth of Fatima, the site in Portugal of many alleged miracles. For $10 you can buy this good luck charm together with certificate of authenticity for your personal miracle of health, wealth, love, etc. A portion of the ad reads, "You receive the GOLDEN CROSS OF FATIMA, and almost immediately you become a 'winner' — winning at bingo, at the lottery, at the race track, at casinos, (wherever you go, you hit the jackpot!)." Of course there is the disclaimer: "The question is, when will these things REALLY happen to you? It depends on you. It depends if you're ready for a Miracle. It depends if you REALLY want a Miracle."

If your lucky cross brings your miracle, you are supposed to write and get it inscribed in their "Good Works Book." The ad includes some quotations from "winners" reports, but none have names "revealed."

Lottery Players Magazine (LPM), had a similar advertisement by the same company but with a New York address instead of New Jersey. This time the "hallowed earth" is in a medal instead of a cross, but with similar claims and disclaimers. The other difference was a place on the order blank for your signature, promising to "report" your miracle.

Is Fatima not your favorite miracle? Maybe it's Lourdes. If so, you can spend $15 for a gold and diamond cross with "genuine" holy water from Lourdes. In the same issue of LPM you'll find a similar ad with different address, same claims, same disclaimers, same promise of report required.

This "entrepreneur" is covering all bases. And he's getting rich on other people's silly superstitions. I don't know how much "hallowed ground" there is at Fatima, or "holy water" at Lourdes, but if these charms work it may turn into a big "hole" and the waters of Lourdes may run "dry."

One avid video poker player from the Orient was sitting next to a lady in a Las Vegas casino whose quarter machine was paying four-of-a-kind every few minutes. Her own machine was "cold" and she remarked about her neighbor's "hot" machine. They struck up a conversation and the lucky lady from Tennessee, the heart of the Bible Belt, pulled out her lucky "charm."

"Here, rub the tummy of my lucky Buddha," she offered.

"Why not," replied the Oriental lady, who was a Catholic and somewhat sceptical of this lucky charm. She shrugged and stroked the chubby tummy. About one minute later she hit a royal flush on her "cold" machine. Unfortunately though, she only played four coins instead of five and received $250.00 instead of $1,000.00. Oh, ye of little faith! A Bible Belt Buddhist and an Oriental Christian — now there's a pair to draw to!

In case you haven't guessed, that "lucky Búddha" is also available in some magazine ad for ten bucks, probably from the same guy or a copycat capitalist.

That same Oriental lady also stated that she never takes her winnings from the tray until she is ready to quit playing. Her husband, who stated that he's not the least bit superstitious, often reaches into his wife's tray to "borrow" her lucky coins. His money always runs out first and he claims he can never win until he plays with "her" money.

Lucky Clothes

"Something borrowed, something blue." Every bride tries to follow that custom. An heirloom wedding dress, veil or piece of jewelry and a "blue garter" are favorites.

One lady player reported that she had attended a wedding at the Circus Circus chapel and was still wearing white gloves when she stopped to drop a few coins in a machine. She hit a jackpot and has never failed since to wear white gloves when she plays. She buys about five pairs a year because the coins turn them black so fast and they wear out from washing so often. When her gloves get dirty, the machine goes "cold." So if she intends to play for very long, she carries a spare pair in her purse.

Then there are the "little old ladies" in tennis shoes and black gloves. When Gamex Industries had their slot machines on trial at Caesars Palace, the jackpot was hit twice in the same month. That's right! Each time it was a different lady, but she was wearing the "tennies" and black gloves. It got to be a standing joke at Gamex that these "little old ladies" would surely hit their machines.

The "same clothes" theory is common with gamblers as well as with many sportsmen like golfers and bowlers.

We know a bowler whose game was consistent and high until he took his dirty bowling towel home and had it washed. His game went into a terrible slump until his towel turned black again from wiping the oil off the bowling ball. Then his slump ended. The towel is still black and so old and ragged it's about half the size of when he started, but he refuses to get a new one.

One amateur golfer who was good enough to have joined the professional tour, wore a favorite pair of yellow trousers in every tournament. They got pretty threadbare over the years and his wife finally threw them out. He swears his golf game has never been the same since.

A fisherman walked out into a mountain stream. After about a half hour without a nibble his waders sprung a leak. As his feet and legs turned cold from the water seeping in, a big trout struck his line. He reeled in the biggest trout he ever caught. Did he buy new waders? Not on your life. He kept bringing home the limit and suffering through the bad colds afterwards.

In Lottery Players Magazine another enterprising salesman combined the lucky clothes and the lucky number superstitions to make his own fortune. He advertises a "Lucky Tee shirt." It carries a chart of scientifically arranged numbers on the back. Someone is supposed to "scratch your back" until you feel the "itchy urge" to say "Stop." The number you call "stop" on is supposed to be lucky. The theory claimed is that the mind sends signals to your back when the lucky number is "scratched."

And people actually buy these things?

Astrology, Horoscopes, and Biorhythms

Many players wear or carry a charm that includes the zodiac sign for their birth month.

Casinos, recognizing the superstitions of players, also cater to them and capitalize on as many as possible. Slot machines often have the lower "logo" glass displayed with zodiac signs, names and shapes of states, or pictures of other symbols of luck.

Many newspapers and magazines run syndicated columns with horoscopes which are extremely popular with gamblers and non-gamblers alike. These horoscopes often include advice on financial, romantic and practical matters that are supposed to be influenced by the stars. And advertisements abound, in gaming magazines especially, that offer your "personal horoscope" with lucky and unlucky days identified to help you with your "game plans."

Some players believe in their personal biorhythm charts, which track the days of the month that are supposed to be most lucky, unlucky or neutral on a scale of one to five, one to ten, or whatever. These biorhythms are charted for the emotional, intellectual and physical ups and downs. When all three lines converge on a high point of the chart on a given day, you're on a "triple high," supposedly your luckiest day. (That's probably the day you go out and get hit by a truck!)

One player we interviewed believes in biorhythms so strongly that she only gambles on triple high days and claims to win consistently. On "triple low" days she won't even leave the house. She also claims to be part "gypsy" and, therefore, somewhat psychic about her luck. When she goes to a casino, she wanders around until a machine "winks" at her.

Right.

Give and Ye Shall Receive

One man was playing video poker with no luck while a Mexican lady beside him was winning something almost every hand. She hit four-of-a-kind, and while the machine was paying, she scooped up a handful of coins, gave them to the change girl, and threw another handful into his tray.

He was shocked at such generosity from a complete stranger.

"What are you doing?" he protested.

"When I win, I always give some away. Then I keep winning. Maybe they'll be lucky for you," she replied.

A few minutes later she hit "4's" again and repeated the "giveaway." The gentleman played the "free" coins and bought more from the change girl. Twice more the Mexican lady hit "4's" and continued to "feed" the loser whose luck didn't change. Then she hit a Royal Flush. She tipped the change girl and the floorman twenty dollars each, filled a coin cup full, threw the last dozen or so coins in the loser's tray and walked away. The loser played those few coins and on the last five finally hit four-of-a-kind. Did he give any away? Nope. He played them all back and left, a loser.

One religious player reported that she cannot win unless she contributes more than her "tithe" to the church on Sunday. After church she has brunch at one of the casino-hotels and then plays slots. If she doesn't contribute extra at church, she doesn't win. If she gives extra, she wins and the amount of her win is anywhere from ten to several hundred times the "extra" contribution. She developed her "system" or "belief" even further. She tries to contribute the "extra" money from at least 10% of her winnings each time. She confesses that these calculations are not *always* correct and she doesn't win *every* time she uses this approach. But this method makes her slot playing enjoyable and she doesn't feel "guilty" about gambling.

Numerology

What's your lucky number? Most people answered this

question by naming their birthday or a portion of it. Most popular numbers given otherwise were 3 and 7.

Special significance (good or bad luck) has been attached to different numbers probably since man first learned to count the dinosaurs or his children. Numbers become special because of association with a particular event, place, or personality. Some take on universal meanings and some have multiple meanings. Some are positive, some are negative, and some are both depending on the individual or the group attributing the magical power.

For instance, three has much religious significance such as the Trinity (Father, Son, and Holy Ghost). Jonah was in the belly of the whale three days; Christ arose from the grave in three days. On the other hand, three cigarettes lit on a match is considered unlucky. "Three's a crowd," and sneezes, deaths, or disasters seem to occur in threes. The first slot machine had three reels, and that number of reels is still the most popular on today's variety of machines.

Four is a "whole" number. We have four seasons, four winds, four main compass points, Four Freedoms, and four suits in a deck of cards.

Five is often associated with Satanism and witchcraft. Pentagrams and pentangles are used in secret rites.

Six and twelve are symbolic to Jews and Christians alike. There are six points on the Star of David, twelve tribes of Israel (named for the twelve sons of Jacob), twelve days of Christmas, twelve months in the year, and twelve signs of the zodiac. Many products are measured by the dozen. But in gaming, two sixes or twelve (boxcars) in craps is a loser on the come-out roll.

Thirteen is considered unlucky by many, but people born on the 13th consider it lucky. After all, there's not much they can do about it. Many hotels are built without a floor numbered 13, but a baker's dozen is 13, better than an "even" dozen. Thirteen original American colonies were first represented with thirteen stars on the flag, but are now represented by thirteen stripes. In a deck of cards there are 13 cards in each suit rather than 14, because the ace counts as the "number 1" as well as the high card in most games. Always remember this double duty card if you play video poker or 21.

Seven is especially symbolic with both positive and negative attributes. The world was created in seven days (six really, God rested on the seventh). There are seven deadly sins, seven virtues, seven seas, seven continents, seven hills of Rome, seven wonders of the world, seven angels in the Book of Revelations, and seven days in a week. Numbers on opposite sides of a dice always add up to seven and all sides then total twenty-one. Twenty-one, a multiple of seven, is the winning hand in the game of blackjack or "twenty-one." It also seems appropriate as well as ironic that there are 21 different meetings of Gamblers Anonymous in Las Vegas.

If you line up 3, 4, or 5 sevens on most slot machines, you will have received a small miracle, and if the jackpot is big enough, you could be in Seventh Heaven. But 7-card stud poker machines were a bust. Probably not because of superstition, but because fewer people are familiar with the game and don't care to lose money trying to learn it from a machine.

Slot players often look for a machine containing as many of their lucky numbers as possible. Others will avoid a machine with the number 13 or any other number they consider especially unlucky. Some players look for machines whose numbers match their street address, apartment number, or their hotel room number. Other players look for a progressive jackpot whose total contains their lucky numbers. Some players will play on days of the week or month that they consider lucky and refuse to play on those they consider unlucky.

Bigotry and Prejudice

Believe it or not, some players transfer their personal prejudices (based on race, sex, age, nationality, etc.) into a superstition about luck. Some forms of this transfer are:

"I won't buy change from _____ change persons because I can't win with it."

"I never play a machine next to a _____ player. If one starts playing next to me, my luck goes bye-bye! I move on immediately, before I lose my luck."

"I never play a machine _____ has been playing. It would definitely be unlucky."

This type of superstition is absurd. Again, machines are not influenced by "who" plays them. Also, the way one machine is being played (whether it's paying or not) has no effect on the adjacent machine being played.

Other Superstitions

We were playing quarter poker one day without any luck. When we bought more quarters, the change girl told us about one of her steady customers who frequently plays quarter poker. She buys coins from this "favorite" change girl only and will accept only rolls of quarters that have "heads" showing at each end of the roll. She claims she can't win if she accepts rolls with "tails" showing at either or both ends.

So the change girl picked out rolls with "heads" for us to see if our luck would change. It didn't. Maybe we should have tried rolls with two "tails," and sort of test the old adage, "one man's meat is another man's poison." But we didn't think the theory worth losing any more money on. *When you're on a losing streak don't keep losing, expecting your luck to change. Quit and try another time.*

Several players stated that they consider it bad luck for a person who is losing or has lost to *touch* their machine. They fear that the bad luck will somehow turn their hot machine cold. Others believe the reverse. If they are losing, they may ask another winner to rub their machine or touch their hands to pass on the good luck. Then there are those who will refuse to "pass on" the good luck in this manner for fear they will lose it. Still others believe that if they don't pass it on and share their luck, they will lose it. Athletes very often "give each other five," to accept or give congratulations for a good performance (i.e. a strike in bowling, home run, basketball score, touchdown, etc.) but also to "pass it on."

Several players said they never play when there is a full moon. Others will not play during the dark phase of the moon. It might be interesting to check if the moon is full or is waxing or waning when all the big jackpots were hit, just to see if there is any "coincidence." We didn't think it worth the time it would take to do so.

Does the weather affect luck or the operation of the machines? Some players think so:

"If it's a gloomy day I stay away."

"When the sun shines, I feel good and I usually have good luck."

"I never play when it's raining. It always puts a damper on my luck. One day my machine was really paying off.

I was near the door and looked out to see it suddenly start raining. My machine never paid another nickel.''

Said another, ''I like to play when it's raining outside. It cheers me up and I seem to have better luck, especially during thunderstorms. Maybe it's the electrical energy in the air that affects the machines, but for me they seem to pay out more then.''

We don't believe that the weather has any effect on the machines. Most players couldn't care less about the weather when they gamble. One July a flash flood washed away 300 cars from Caesars Palace parking lot. Across the street at the Flamingo, players were standing in flood waters creeping into the casino, pulling those handles as if nothing were wrong.

What is even more frightening is to see players calmly plunking in coins while smoke and fire alarms are blaring at deafening levels. They appear confident that the noise is ''just a test'' whether announced or not. Many players think such alarms are merely the sound of a jackpot being hit. There was a period after the disastrous MGM and Hilton fires in Las Vegas the same year when players would run for the doors at any noise resembling a fire alarm, but how soon they forget!

Superstition will always play a major role in gambling. Try to influence the Goddess Fortuna to spin her wheel in your favor, trust to blind luck, or believe in charms and spells, whatever you wish. We have to concede that ''Luck'' often defies logic, especially with slot machine playing.

If we said otherwise, who would believe us?

CHAPTER 12

Manufacturers

A Brief History

Credit for introducing the crazy contraption called a slot machine is given to Charles Fey. The San Francisco Chronicle of April 15, 1887 describes it:

"A group of owners of Saloon and Restaurants of Market, Mission, Embarkadera and Barbary Coast gathered this morning in the small machine shop of Charley Fey at 631 Howard St. to view Mr. Fey's entirely new Liberty Bell, a machine featuring 3 reels mostly hidden with Horseshoes, Spades,

Diamonds, Hearts, and Bells symbols on the reels. The device is operated by depositing a nickel in a slot to release the handle. When the right combination of symbols stop in the window, the player is awarded coins ranging from 2 on 2 Horseshoes to 20 for 3 Bells. Most of those present agreed the machine should be a great success.''

That last line turned out to be the understatement of the century between the machine's introduction in 1887 and the phenomenal importance of slots in the gaming industry today. Incidentally, one meaning of the word ''fey'' is ''clairvoyant, visionary.'' It certainly fits Charles Fey, the inventor.

Interesting to note is the influence of poker on the colored ''payout'' on Fey's machine:

Three Bells	10 drinks
Flush of Hearts	8 drinks
Flush of Diamonds	6 drinks
Flush of Spades	4 drinks
Two Horseshoes and Star	2 drinks
Two Horseshoes	1 drinks

Although the chart listed drinks as the reward, the machine actually paid out nickels as noted in the ''Chronicle.'' Since Fey used playing card symbols on his reels, he also bought the Federal Tax stamp for his machine to cover the two cent Federal revenue tax on each deck of playing cards. Incidentally, the Federal revenue tax on gaming devices was repealed on July 1, 1980.

Fey did not sell his machines but placed them in the gambling saloons on a 50 percent rental basis, thereby becoming the first slot route operator as well as inventor and manufacturer.

Forty-two years later in 1929, Fey also built the first slot machine to take a silver dollar. That machine featured three reels with fruit and bar symbols and a top jackpot of $100.

Both machines built by Fey are currently on display at the Liberty Bell Saloon and Restaurant in Reno, Nevada, which is run by Fey's grandsons, Marshall and Franklin Fey.

Fey's success was unchallenged by other manufacturers until one of his machines disappeared from the marketplace and later appeared at Herbert Mills' factory where it was thoroughly dissected and obviously used as the model for Mills' "Operators Bell" machine. Mills, who manufactured arcade machines in Chicago, produced the "Operators Bell" machine in 1910. Because its case was made of iron, it was nicknamed "The Iron Case." Mills' machine had 20 symbols (bars, bells, plums, cherries, and lemons) per reel whereas Fey's had only 10. Mills' machine also had a larger window so that three lines of symbols (nine total) could be seen. But payout was on the three center line symbols only. It should have been called the "teaser" or "carrot" because you could see the winning symbols you just missed and might catch on the next spin. That "carrot" dangling before the eyes of the proverbial jackass player kept him plunking coins into machines whose average payout was only about 50%. There were no gaming regulations in those days and machines were shipped all over the country. And that "teaser" or "carrot" became standard in the industry and is definitely part of the continuing "lure" that keeps players trying "just one more coin" again and again and again "*ad infinitum.*"

Mills started his company in 1889 with his "Three For One" machine. This simple slot consisted of three coin tubes. When you dropped in a coin, it would roll down one of the three tubes. If it rolled into the winning tube, you won three coins for one. If it rolled into the other tubes, you lost. Mills refined that machine into the "Owl" and later the "Dewey" named for the Spanish-American war hero. Both machines were so successful that he was able to finance a string of arcades from the Midwest to New York. Some of his arcade machines were grip testers, weight lifters, peep movies, fortune tellers and music boxes. One of the music boxes combined the playing of a violin and a piano and became an international success. One was purchased by Kaiser Wilhelm. Incidentally, the "Dewey" machine can be seen in the Gambling Museum at the Stardust Hotel-Casino in Las Vegas, along with many other antique slots and arcade machines.

Meanwhile, an associate of Mills, O.D. Jennings, split from Mills and formed his own company in 1906. His company introduced the first electrically powered slot machine called the "Electrojax" in 1931. Even though it was a popular novelty at first, it was not a complete success because players did not trust automation.

Jennings produced his "Little Duke" in 1933 with its candy vending attachment on the side and the "Duchess Vendor" in 1934 with the candy dispenser built directly into the machine. Incidentally, since gambling was illegal at the time, many early slot machines included these gum or candy attachments to circumvent the anti-gambling laws. When the candy dispenser became empty, the machine would not play. To keep from having to refill the candy dispenser, many owners soaked the gum or candy rolls in kerosene. Players soon learned not to turn the lever to collect the candy. The practice was harmless but "distasteful" in more ways than one, but kept the machines operative and profitable.

Many of these early machines were used as "trade stimulators" rather than gambling devices. Merchants would sometimes allow the winnings to be exchanged for merchandise such as cigars, cigarettes, drinks, etc. Where else do you think "close, but no cigar" came from. Now we have green stamps, bingo games, sweepstakes, drawings, and other premiums offered at the gas stations, the supermarkets and the fast-food joints throughout the country. Now arcade games are for amusement only with prizes to winners being additional "free" games. Sound familiar? The most common prize on a lottery ticket is another "free ticket" which usually turns out to be another loser.

Jennings' "Duchess Vendor" was a very compact machine, making it easy to move around and hide when a police raid or gambling crack-down was imminent. The same year he produced the "Century Vendor" with two forerunners of today's popular machines — optional coinage and player's skill. A braking button under each reel could be pushed to stop the reel at the player's discretion. A year later Jennings introduced "The Chief" with the format that became basic in the industry for the next 30 years. Its Indian Head logo became the symbol for all Jennings slot machines. It also included a "slug rejector" and an anti-overlap coin return device, both deterrents to cheating.

Other innovations by Jennings were the first multi-line machine (Tic-Tac-Toe) in 1951 which paid on two diagonal lines as well as three straight lines, and the popular four-reel (Buckaroo) introduced in 1960.

In 1954 the Jennings company was purchased by TJM

Corporation which combined three big names in slot machines at that time, Jennings, Mills and J. H. Kinney, maker of a console-type machine. Ultimately these companies and rights to trademarks were purchased by OTX Corporation which later changed its name to the Mills-Jennings Company. It was then sold in 1980 to private individuals. The products produced by the current company bear no resemblance or direct relationship to the original products.

Today's Major Manufacturers

The major manufacturers of slot machines are Bally Manufacturing (Bally) and International Game Technology (IGT). With their fingers in all aspects of gaming, it's no wonder they occupy the top ranks in their industry. They are first in production, sales and distribution of slot machines and other gaming paraphernalia in the U.S. and are rapidly gaining ground in the world-wide market.

Bally is one of the oldest manufacturers of slot machines, but it also owns casinos in Atlantic City, Reno, and Las Vegas. It owns several health spas and the Six Flags theme parks around the country. At this writing, Bally had agreed to sell the seven Six Flags parks for $450 million. This sale reduced their debt of $350 million and gave them $100 million profit on this venture alone. They were also negotiating to sell the health spas.

On the other hand, IGT is a relatively new corporation enjoying phenomenal prosperity. Its history begins with a veteran in the gaming industry, William S. "Si" Redd. Redd built and ran Bally Distributing in Nevada for years.

In the 70's, Walt Fraley of Fortune Coin Company in

Las Vegas, created one of the first successful lines of video machines. At the same time Si Redd founded A-1 Supply in 1975, in Reno, Nevada. A-1 Supply was also working on a poker slot machine. In 1979, Redd bought Fortune Coin and combined it with A-1 Supply into a new company called "Sircoma" for <u>SI</u> <u>R</u>edd <u>CO</u>in <u>MA</u>chines. In 1981, he established International Game Technology (IGT) and opened stock for public purchase and trade. IGT's main manufacturing facility is in Reno but it still maintains a facility in Las Vegas for sales and service.

At a recent International Gaming Exposition, IGT had the largest display. Their video poker machines are certainly the "success story" of the industry, rapidly becoming the number one game for slot players.

Electronic Data Technology (EDT) is a wholly-owned IGT subsidiary based in Las Vegas. It specializes in gaming software, player tracking data and slot information systems for casinos (described under Slot Promotions), mechanical ticket dispensing machines and other gaming related equipment.

(This co-author worked in the engineering department of Sircoma and was instrumental in the computer programming of the video slots and video pokers. Later, as a consultant he helped EDT develop the credit-card bonus and player tracking system installed in a number of casinos. In 1974 he designed one of the first slot monitoring systems for Gamex Industries.)

IGT owns a substantial equity in Syntech International, Inc. supplying equipment for the mushrooming lottery business. It also has an exclusive distributorship agreement with Atlantic City Coin and Slot Service Company handling sales and service not only in New Jersey but in other areas of the world market. With the re-legalization of slot machines in Puerto Rico, they recently sold 675 IGT machines to the Puerto Rico Tourism Company. IGT also has a major manufacturing/assembly plant in Sydney, Australia.

IGT, the brainchild of Si Redd, has been successful in capturing the majority of the video gaming machine market. Redd entered into a unique written agreement for five years with Bally that gave IGT exclusive rights to the manufacture and sale of video machines. In return, IGT agreed not to manufacture reel type machines, Bally's largest line. Consequently, the introduction of the video slots and especially the video poker machines which became so popular had little competition in Nevada.

In Atlantic City, however, gaming regulations prohibited a manufacturer from supplying more than 50% of the machines in any one casino. Because of Si Redd's ties with Bally, Atlantic City counted IGT machines in Bally's 50% limitation. After a lot of legal maneuvering, IGT was finally considered a separate manufacturer and allowed to place its machines in the Atlantic City casinos independent of Bally's 50%.

The agreement between Bally and IGT ran out in 1984. Bally is now producing its own line of video slots and poker machines. They provide interesting varieties of choices for players but have not yet received the wide popularity enjoyed by IGT's machines. However, Bally was recently awarded a $7.5 million contract to provide video poker machines (their 5000 series) for the U.S. Army and Air Force bases in Germany, Korea, and Japan. The order was for 2,300 units. That's about $3,260 per machine. Don't worry about your tax dollars though. The purchase was made from non-appropriated funds, that is, revenue from military personnel exchange stores and clubs.

Si Redd started his career with a coin-operated jukebox and amusement machine route in the South which he expanded into the Midwest and New England. Moving to Nevada in 1967, he became a major distributor of slot machines and gaming devices. In a Las Vegas Sun article, Redd was referred to as the state's "slot machine king" and the "father of video gaming."

According to John Morrisey, in Las Vegas Business Press, IGT has placed over 45,000 gaming machines around the world in the past twelve years. They manufactured nearly 10,000 machines last year alone. Morrisey quotes Charles Mathewson, IGT's president, telling of IGT's phenomenal success: "The company was founded by a real genius in the gaming machine business, (referring to Si Redd) I don't know how else to say it. He was innovative with a lot of new ideas. Ten years ago, there were 40,000 to 45,000 slot machines in Nevada. Now there are more than 100,000 and they produce more than half of the state's gaming revenues."

Because of the booming slot machine business, new manufacturers are entering the market every year and many older manufacturers are developing new lines. Some of the new machines introduced at a recent Gaming Exposition in Las Vegas are covered briefly in the section describing the different types of machines. Besides IGT and Bally, prominent exhibitors at the show included Games of Nevada; Sigma Game, Inc.; Status Game Corporation; and Aristocrat, an Australian firm trying to open a market in the United States.

Sigma Game, Inc. is a Japanese owned and based company that is rapidly expanding its field. Along with its slots and version of video poker, it has "Sigma Derby" the most successful horse racing machine, which is described elsewhere. Sigma's holding corporation purchased the former Holiday International Casino in downtown Las Vegas. That large casino-hotel had been closed for several years, and after a $15 million renovation it reopened as the Park Hotel-Casino.

Another Japanese owned company, Universal, is making great strides in the casino market with its slot machines. It offers something that other manufacturers do not, that is, casino layout and a total promotional concept which most casinos normally do with their own personnel.

Casino Electronics, Inc. (CEI), another up and coming manufacturer, produces 21, Keno and Video Poker machines. It has also received approval from the Gaming Board to manufacture a new line of slots called ''Hot Slots'' featuring 15 different varieties. CEI is a sister to United Coin Company, one of the largest slot route operators in Nevada, which places machines in establishments with restricted licenses. Gaming and Technology is the financial parent of CEI and United Coin.

New companies, old companies, mergers, and splits, you name it. The manufacture of gaming devices appears to be so lucrative that many inexperienced entrepreneurs enter the field and are soon plowed under by the veterans in the industry. Only a few reap the golden harvest. Trying to include all of them here is beyond the scope and purpose of this book.

CHAPTER 13

Slots' Place in the Big Picture

The Magnitude of Gaming Revenues

The "Slot Machine Mania" that has developed over the past few years is clearly reflected in the overall statistics for gaming revenue. Although statistics are usually boring, you'll be amazed at what you are about to read. The magnitude of dollars spent on legal gambling is awesome. Some of the revenue figures we are about to cite are almost incomprehensible.

Winnings for all Nevada casinos increase every year and now have reached 3.9 Billion Dollars! That's the casino's *winnings.* Or put another way...all the players' *losses.*

In Clark County (Las Vegas), the total gross gaming revenue for 1986 is approximately 2.4 billion dollars, of which 53 million is paid in taxes to the state. In Washoe County (Reno) the gross gaming revenue is almost 656 million dollars. That tells you where the most action is.

Since gaming started in Atlantic City in 1978 the eight percent tax on each casino's gross winnings has resulted in over $1 billion to the casino revenue fund, which is used to finance programs for senior and disabled citizens of the state. In 1978, contributions from gaming were $10.7 million; today, $190.9 million!

Slots Vs. Table Games

Slot and video game playing accounts for 54 percent of the revenue in Las Vegas, "a percentage roughly equal to that of Atlantic City." This is an increase in slot playing from about 35 percent in the early 1980's in Las Vegas. The distribution was already equally balanced in Atlantic City.

In Laughlin, Nevada, slots account for *more than 70 percent of the win!* A bridge built by Laughlin across the Colorado river to Bullhead City, Arizona, makes for a quicker trip across the state line for many Arizona "Sunbirds" with their rolls of coins ready for the "win" column...the casino's win column.

From the 441 slots this year at McCarran Airport in Las Vegas comes $11 million in winnings. Of that total 76.1% goes to the county for airport projects and 23.9% to concessionaire Michael Gaughan who maintains and foots all expenses and taxes out of his 23.9%. Michael Gaughan is also the principle owner of the Barbary Coast and Gold Coast Casino-Hotels.

According to Thomas D. Elias in the Las Vegas Sun, table games provided more than 80 percent of casino income in 1967. Today, *56 percent* of Nevada casino proceeds came from machines of various types. Also, Charles Lombardo, assistant manager for slots at Bally's stated, "The take from table games is stagnant, craps is even down. Slot players are the gamblers of the future. The Space Invaders generation has arrived."

As you can see from the following table comparing revenues for table games and slots, only on the Las Vegas Strip do table games show a higher percentage than slots. From early indications and our observation of the recent changes in the Strip casinos, we think that percentage will probably fall in line with the other areas as new figures come in.

COMPARISON OF REVENUE FOR TABLE GAMES (includes keno and bingo) and COIN OPERATED DEVICES

STATE OF NEVADA — FISCAL YEAR 1987 (for Locations with $1,000,000 and over)

LOCATION AND # OF CASINOS	TABLE GAMES				COIN OPERATED DEVICES			
	AVE. AREA SQ. FT.	REV PER SQ. FT.	TOTAL REVENUE	PCT. OF TOTAL	AVE. AREA SQ. FT.	REV PER SQ. FT.	TOTAL REVENUE	PCT. OF TOTAL
CLARK COUNTY								
LV STRIP (38)	9,004	2,559	806,342,175	50.5	15,675	1,233	716,438,492	44.8
LV DOWNTOWN (21)	8,416	1,325	189,630,216	36.2	13,845	1,062	308,879,216	58.9
BOULDER HWY/ (8) HENDERSON	6,563	401	18,408,205	19.5	10,885	944	73,152,665	77.7
LAUGHLIN (6)	5,827	1,250	43,715,750	20.8	16,724	1,595	160,016,869	76.2
OTHER COUNTIES								
LAKE TAHOE (6)	9,952	2,417	144,340,512	48.3	22,258	1,083	144,647,941	48.3
ELKO (12)	3,653	596	26,106,751	31.7	6,049	753	54,635,540	66.4
WENDOVER (5)	4,125	706	14,563,883	33.5	7,492	751	28,121,289	64.6
RENO/SPARKS (30)	6,520	1,134	199,565,681	32.7	14,296	942	390,393,580	63.9
REST OF NEV. (34)	2,978	654	58,512,490	23.4	5,455	1,015	158,733,821	73.5
TOTAL STATE OF NEVADA (155)	6,486	1,637	1,486,622,359	40.5	12,238	1,098	2,031,898,124	55.4

Source: State of Nevada Gaming Abstract, 1987.

What has caused the shift in revenues from tables to slots? According to "Gaming and Wagering Business" magazine one reason is that the new federal regulations that require reporting of all winnings over $10,000 to the Internal Revenue Service has marked an end to the "catered to high-roller era." The high rollers were traditionally table game gamblers. Now the million dollar slot jackpots are pulling former table players to the slot area. Besides offering huge jackpots, casinos have instituted more marketing plans to attract slot players. Richard Schuetz, executive vice president for casino operations at the Frontier was quoted in the *Las Vegas Sun*: "There has always been heavy competition among casinos for the table players. Now the same competition is starting for slot players."

According to Elias, the switch from table games to electronic games has increased the casinos' take and allowed the big hotels to cut expenses. Schuetz confirms his opinion, "Our poker machines produce more than 10 times the take of our cardroom. We've taken out a pit that once had eight table games and we're making more money than ever. That's let us cut down labor costs while still pleasing our customers."

We wish we could offer stats on the revenue generated from residents of Las Vegas as compared to that from tourists. But that would be impossible to compile. However, income from tourism would undoubtedly be higher or the hotels wouldn't be adding more rooms.

According to Rossi Rolenkatter, Director of Tourism and Research for the Las Vegas Convention and Visitor Authority (LVCVA), a record 1,633,019 people visited Las Vegas in March 1987, representing a 10.3 percent increase over March 1986. That's for just *one* winter month in

Vegas. Also, despite the addition of 3,000 hotel rooms during the first quarter of 1987, the occupancy rate was 99.2 percent on weekends. Conventions aside, that's a bunch of people taking a trip for a "gambling high."

We can't begin to calculate the percentage of those visitors who went home losers instead of winners. We'll bet most of them experienced a "low" rather than a "high," especially in their pocketbooks.*

Las Vegas attracts some of the largest conventions in the world to the Convention Center just one block from the Strip and to Cashman Field Center just north of Glitter Gulch. However, despite several expansions to the Convention Center, the larger conventions still rely on the convention halls in the surrounding hotels to provide additional exhibit space and seminar rooms. Attracting conventions to Las Vegas gives people "two" or more reasons to visit the city. First, a business related convention helps fill up all the hotel rooms. Second, people who might never "plan" to visit Las Vegas otherwise frequently fall in love with its many attractions and return again and again to gamble, see the celebrity shows, or relax in its resort atmosphere.

According to Ralenkotter, more tourists now visit Las Vegas. Of the whopping 15.2 million people last year, 1.5 million attended conventions, expositions, and other gatherings hosted by the city. That figure represents a 41.7 percent increase over the prior year. CONEXPO, the convention for the construction industry and its equipment manufacturers has 112,600 delegates alone, to fill 61,000 hotel rooms!

Some statistics show that of the convention visitors, a

---

*Most casino executives believe the percentage of losers is greater than 95%! A sobering statistic indeed!

much larger majority play slots than the typical gambler. Not surprisingly, those who visit Las Vegas primarily to gamble are table players. Those who are in town for a convention are not necessarily crap shooters or blackjack counters. Indeed, their gambling fever, for the most part, is low. So the slot machines get most of the action.

As for Atlantic City visitors, the traffic is bumper to bumper on the Garden State Parkway, often worse than that on the notorious Los Angeles freeways. In the casinos, you have to stand in line behind players for a seat at a table or to play a slot machine.

Also, the visitors to Atlantic City usually do not stay as long as those to Nevada. It is just a few hours drive from highly populated cities and many players arrive on buses or drive in for a day's entertainment.

Atlantic City is a former resort with a tattered elegance, remnants of a past splendor. When gaming was legalized there, it was expected to revitalize the city as a whole. The great success of the casinos has yet to spill over into the rest of the city. Instead, it has developed only islands of opulence, casinos that are bright bustling, happy places, in a sea of crumbling buildings graying like driftwood on the beach.

Are Slots Taking Over the Casino?

Recognizing that slots are a threat to the existence of the traditional casino table games, casinos have started to try to keep the two in balance. Along with slot tournaments, they are holding more frequent tournaments for blackjack, craps and poker with higher stakes than ever before. Especially on the LV Strip, casinos try to add table games in proportion to expansion for slot machines, to keep the total gaming concept alive, but the evidence is hard to find. Perhaps the pendulum will swing back again, but we doubt it.

Why? If you walk into a casino at 3 or 4 a.m. you will find most tables shut down, but many slot machines will still be jingling away. Casinos are routinely converting lounges, bars, keno parlors, coffee shops — any space they can find — into . . . you guessed it, more rows and rows of slots. Today, slots are where the "real" action is!

CHAPTER 14

The Future Of Slots

On The Drawing Board

A few of the giant casino-hotels will soon become "super giants" in their race to be the "biggest and the best" in the U.S.A. if not the world.

Plans have been unveiled for a new 3,600 room hotel to be built on the Las Vegas Strip, rivaling all the rest. Price tag for the 86 acres it will need was $56 million. Estimated cost of the new resort is $500 million!

And yet another casino/hotel is going up a few blocks south with 3,000 more rooms! Do you think that the other giants will stand idly by as these "super structures" reach for the sky? No sir! Many of the other major hotels have announced expansions that could possibly total another 5,000 rooms!

Bally's (former MGM) has 2,830 rooms and at this writing has razed the adjacent motel to make room for what? Another tower expansion? We'll bet on it!

The El Rancho is planning a 587 room tower and the Rivera is adding 757 and received approval for a high rise expansion for a total of 4,179 that is supposed to make it the largest privately owned hotel in the world. Other hotels on the list for expansions or new construction include the Dunes, Holiday Inn, Imperial Palace, Sahara, Golden Nugget, and Southstar.

Although not official, the Flamingo Hilton is expected to expand soon with as many as 1,600 rooms making *it* the largest with 4,527.

What about the other giant on the "magic corner" of Flamingo and Las Vegas Blvd? Caesars Palace has already revealed its intention to build a Roman Forum on the north side of its mammoth complex. The "Forum" will include a 150-store shopping complex sure to rival the exclusive shops in the Fashion Show Mall down the street. Our guess is that the shops inside the main hotel will then make way for more... *slot machines!*

Also planned are two open air pits, that can be seen from the sidewalk, which will show everything from Gladiator matches to wild animal acts. Christians, watch out! Rome may rise again!

The Strip will likely have another "new kid on the block" to contend with if plans continue for the Southstar hotel-casino complex to be built south of the Hacienda Hotel. Southstar is conceived as nine high-rise hotels totalling 6,000 rooms built around a central diamond-shaped casino of 120,000 square feet, which would be the state's largest. The hotels are the vision of Southstar Development Corporation, a group of successful California and Nevada real estate developers. Construction of the casino complex is the responsibility of Allison and Associates, headed by Don Allison, former president of Caesars Palace. The entire resort will include a 2,000 seat showroom, retail shops, multi-tiered parking garage, gourmet restaurants and convention facilities. Prices will range from "affordable to plush."

Kirk Kerkorian, builder of the original MGM Grand, is back in the casino business with the purchase of the Desert Inn from Summa Corp. We expect a major expansion of this prime Strip property to include not only more hotel rooms (the DI now has 800) but more "room" for more slot machines!

Because of the increasing convention attendance, the Las Vegas Convention and Visitor Authority predicted that within two years Las Vegas would need to add 10,000 more rooms to its current total of 55,000. If all these proposed superstructures materialize, the 10,000 room estimate may well be exceeded in the race for the top mark in high-rise accommodations.

What will pay for all this construction? If the current trend continues, the revenue from slots and more slots will foot a good part of the bill for their elevation and evolution to "super giant" status.

Meanwhile south of Las Vegas near the California and Arizona borders the town of Laughlin continues to expand. It currently is the fastest growing area in the state, with an airport and three new hotels on the drawing board. That little community was started by Don Laughlin in 1966. By 1987, his Riverside Casino grossed $100 million!

Together with the other five casino/hotels, some of them owned by Circus-Circus, the Boyd Group and the Holiday Inn, Laughlin surpassed Lake Tahoe in gaming revenues with $186 million, in third place behind Las Vegas and Reno. They currently have 3,246 rooms and 6,593 slot machines. Harrah's Del Rio when built will have 479 rooms and 1,013 slot machines. Two other casinos are also planned for that little boomtown on the Colorado River.

A full blown casino is also planned on the Fort Mojave Indian reservation near the California Border southeast of Laughlin. It depends on the congressional decision as to whether or not it will be subject to state gaming regulations.

The Eldorado Hotel/Casino in downtown Reno will add a 25 story 400 room tower and 22,100 square feet more casino space. The expansion will put them in the same league as Harrah's Reno and the Tahoe Nugget.

Who knows, maybe the future will see a high speed train connecting the Reno, Las Vegas, and Laughlin areas so that tourists may visit all three locations in one day. The train may even be equipped with slot machines so travelers can play on the way. This could be a project financed by the Super Giants and the manufacturers so tourists don't lose all that playing time driving their own vehicles for five to ten hours per day.

In Atlantic City, casinos also continue to expand. The Tropicana, renamed "TropWorld" with its 200 million dollar expansion, will have casino space totaling 40,000 square feet! Seventeen restaurants, lounges and food outlets will seat 4,600 people at a time.

Construction of Donald Trump's Taj Mahal will probably continue and when complete could be the largest casino in the world.

Slot Areas for Non-Smokers

The current trend to accommodate non-smoking activities has already started to infiltrate the casino atmosphere. Most restaurants have non-smoking sections. La Mirage in Las Vegas went so far as to ban smoking in the entire restaurant. Some smokers vowed never to return but the lure of the slots is too strong and they have been drifting back.

Most casinos already have posted non-smoking table games. As the non-smoking players continue to outnumber the smokers, more casinos will follow northern Nevada in dividing the slot areas too.

Slots in Hotel Rooms

Why not play from the hotel room, by way of TV monitors and cashless remote accounting? This possibility has already been considered. It would be difficult (though not impossible) to monitor whether or not the machines were being played by minors who may be in the party of guests. The technology does exist to overcome this problem.

Automatic Gambling Against Your Bank Account

Gambling on cashless slots with automatic deductions and additions to credit card or bank accounts is a definite possibility. You might even get periodic print-outs of your "action." Such print-outs would provide a player with excellent records for money management. Safeguards on limitations of "withdrawals" would be necessary to prevent compulsive spending below levels needed for payment of existing loans and monthly expenses, of course. The IRS would love this type of gambling if they could insist that banks automatically report taxes on winnings as they do interest. This could have a positive effect on legislation to allow more tax deductions for losses that exceed your winnings in a given year or for prorating wins and losses over a period of years.

Slot Playing at Home to Win

Casinos might even rent remote monitors or machines for installation at homes, with a selected password to play specific machines on the casino floor, either on a credit card or advance deposit basis. This may not be as crazy as it seems at first. It certainly is technically possible using your telephone or cable lines. Imagine yourself playing your favorite machine from your easy chair or bed at all hours of the day or night, taking time out only to watch Johnny Carson or the Super Bowl. A nice diversion during commercials instead of a trip to the fridge for something fattening.

High Roller Carrels

For the ultimate in sophistication and intimacy for high rollers, why not enclosed booths for one, two, or even four-player parties? Each carrel would contain an assortment of the latest types of slots, video poker, keno, horse racing, etc. (equipped as pre-ordered by the client for his favorite games). In addition, there would be remote monitors for use in placing wagers on the live action from the sports book and keno lounge. The high roller would merely deposit his bank roll with the casino cashier, and his pre-programmed slots could automatically deduct his play and add his winnings for as long as he wishes to play and/or his bankroll lasts. There could be a call button or intercom for beverage and perhaps even meal service with menus on the remote monitor if the player is reluctant to leave his machine for meals as many avid players are.

Does this sound too far out for you? Well, if some people today are willing to plunk down 50 grand per season for a "luxury box" at an NFL stadium, why not a luxury box at their favorite casino?

Where will this slot mania end?

An article with StarDate 11/7/2121 might read:

A SLOT TOURNAMENT FOR THE RICH AND FAMOUS.

Five casino/hotels on separate space stations have announced a five-week tournament of tournaments, the ultimate in posh entertainment for slot high rollers. At an entry fee of a cool million, contestants will spend three days each at Caesars Universe, Astro-Hilton, MGM Constellation, Galaxy Nugget and Bally's Nova, in a weightless but heavily intense round of slot competition, vying for the ultimate prize — a half billion dollars credit at the Intergalatic Bank. Between sessions of tournament play, vacationers will practice on the latest in space-linked slots, The Meteor Shower, with a possible progressive jackpot which started at one trillion dollars and is currently approaching the lucky $13 trillion mark.

It's time to close the book on this madness. Good luck, dear reader!

Bibliography

Gambling and the Law, I. Nelson Rose, Gambling Times, Inc., Hollywood, California 1986

State of Nevada Regulations: Nevada Gaming Commission and State Gaming Control Board, Carson City, Nevada

"In The Pink," Flamingo Hilton Newsletter, Las Vegas, Nevada, October 1987

"Bally's MVP Newsletter," Las Vegas, Nevada Fall 1987

"Atlantic City Casino Association Fact Sheet," Atlantic City, New Jersey, April 1986

"Atlantic City Action," Newsletter, Al Glasgow, Glasco Associates, Inc., Atlantic City, New Jersey, 1986/1987

"Gambling Times," Magazine, Hollywood, California 1986/1987

"Gaming & Wagering Business," BMT Publications, New York, New York 1986/1988

"World Gaming Report," Los Angeles, California 1986/1987

"Nevada Gaming Abstract," State Gaming Control Board, Carson City, Nevada, 1987

"Gaming Nevada Style," Nevada Gaming Commission and State Gaming Control Board, Carson City, Nevada Revised November, 1985

"General Guidelines For Gaming Devices," EG&G, Albuquerque Division, Albuquerque, New Mexico, 7 January 1972

Las Vegas Behind The Tables, Barney Vinson, Gollehon Press, Inc., Grand Rapids, Michigan 1986/1988

Las Vegas Behind The Tables, PART 2, Barney Vinson, Gollehon Press, Inc., Grand Rapids, Michigan 1988

Reno *GAZETTE,* 1984-1986 selected articles

All About Slots and Video Poker, John Gollehon, G.P. Putnam's Sons, New York, New York 1985

Pay the Line, John Gollehon, G.P. Putnam's Sons, New York 1984

Casino Games, John Gollehon, Gollehon Press, Inc., Grand Rapids, Michigan 1986/1988

Scarne's New Complete Guide to Gambling, John Scarne, Simon & Schuster, Inc., New York, New York

The Odds on Virtually Everything, complied by the editors of Heron House, G.P. Putnam's Sons, New York, New York

House of Cards, Jerome H. Skolnick, Little, Brown and Company, Boston, Massachusetts

Las Vegas *SUN* Newspaper, selected articles 1984-1988

Las Vegas *REVIEW-JOURNAL* Newspaper selected articles 1984-1988

"Celebrity Spotlight," Harrah's, Reno, Nevada

"Lottery & Gaming Review," Ames Publications, Inc., Buffalo, New York

228

"Lottery Player's Magazine," Regal Communication Corp., Cherry Hill, New Jersey, 1984-1987

"What's On In Las Vegas," Magazine, Las Vegas, Nevada, 1987

"Casino World," Gromercy Information Services, Inc., New York, New York, 1986

"Compulsive Gambling Only Seven Answers Away," by *Kansas City Star and Times,* reprinted in *Las Vegas Sun,* July 7, 1987

"The Impact of Slot Machine Cheating," Seminar by Dan Reaser, International Gaming Business Exposition, Las Vegas, Nevada, March 3, 1987

"Players Panorama," Newspaper, Las Vegas, Nevada

"Las Vegas Business Press," Las Vegas, Nevada

"Insight On the News," Magazine, Washington, D.C.

Epilogue

Video Poker Update

Since the initial publication of this book, many readers have expressed a desire for more information on video poker, especially the playing strategy. We're happy to oblige with some basic rules and suggestions to help you develop your own strategy.

One thing that's important to mention first, however, is that basic poker strategies for the live game do not always apply to video poker. These strategies must be adjusted to take into account the payoff advantage to the player of a 5-coin (or other maximum coin) Royal Flush. For example, holding two cards to a Royal Flush (with no other win potential to the hand) is generally agreed to be the best strategy because of the Royal Flush jackpot looming so large. But in live poker, this would certainly not be a smart strategy all of the time.

Another thing worth noting is the fact that video poker strategies are not absolutes because of the varying payoffs and skill factors that tend to complicate the determination of exacting percentages or exacting strategies. Plus, many strategies promoted by one "expert" are debated by another. Who's to say. We offer these suggestions that follow with that important understanding in mind.

KEY TO ABBREVIATIONS AND SYMBOLS

Cards: A = ACE   J = JACK
          K = KING   WJ = JOKER (WILD CARD)
          Q = QUEEN   W2 = WILD DEUCE

Winning Hands:

  PAT = A Hand that is an automatic winner without drawing additional cards.

   RF = ROYAL FLUSH (A,K,Q,J,10 OF THE SAME SUIT)

 RFWJ = ROYAL FLUSH WITH JOKER

 RFW2 = ROYAL FLUSH WITH ONE TO 3 DEUCES

 4W2 = FOUR DEUCES (DEUCES WILD MACHINE ONLY)

  5's = FIVE OF A KIND
        (Any combination of same high or numbered card with a Wild Joker or Wild Deuces)

   SF = STRAIGHT FLUSH
        (Five cards in sequence in the same suit)

  4's = FOUR OF A KIND

FH = FULL HOUSE
(Three of a kind with two of a kind)
F = FLUSH
(Five cards of the same suit)
ST = STRAIGHT
(Five cards in sequence not of the same suit)
3's = THREE OF A KIND
2PR = 2 PAIR
JB = PAIR OF JACKS OR HIGHER
KB = PAIR OF KINGS OR HIGHER
E = EVEN MONEY
OS = OTHER SUIT
KICKER = A CARD THAT DOES NOT LOGICALLY
MATCH A TOP HAND.
(e.g. With a pair of kings, don't hold an ace
or any other card to try for a Full House.)

TYPICAL POKER PAYTABLES

Refer to Page 62 for the Rank of Poker Hands (in ascending value). Note that most paytables on machines display the paytables in *descending* order as we have in the following typical paytables for the most frequently played machines without progressive jackpots or special incentive bonuses for maximum coins played.

Nickels:

WINNING HAND	1 COIN	2 COINS	3 COINS	4 COINS	5 COINS
ROYAL FLUSH	250	500	750	1000	4000
STRAIGHT FLUSH	100	200	300	400	500
4 OF A KIND	50	100	150	200	250
FULL HOUSE	12	24	36	48	60
FLUSH	8	16	24	32	40
STRAIGHT	6	12	18	24	30
3 OF A KIND	3	6	9	12	15
2 PAIR	2	4	6	8	10
JACKS OR BETTER	—	—	—	—	—

Quarters & Dollars:

WINNING HAND	1 COIN	2 COINS	3 COINS	4 COINS	5 COINS
ROYAL FLUSH	250	500	750	1000	4000
STRAIGHT FLUSH	50	100	150	200	250
4 OF A KIND	25	50	75	100	125
FULL HOUSE	9	18	27	36	45
FLUSH	6	12	18	24	30
STRAIGHT	4	8	12	16	20
3 OF A KIND	3	6	9	12	15
2 PAIR	2	4	6	8	10
JACKS OR BETTER	1	2	3	4	5

This paytable is typical of non-progressive machines, noting the 9-coin payout for a Full House, and 6-coin payout for a Flush. Usually, progressive machines have a less attractive payout for these winning hands of 8 coins and 5 coins respectively. **Always look for the ''9-6'' machine.**

Joker Poker — 1 Wild Card:

Nickels: 10 Coins Required for Highest Jackpot

WINNING HAND	1 COIN	2-9 COINS	10 COINS
ROYAL FLUSH W/O JOKER	400	MULTIPLY # OF COINS PLAYED BY AMOUNT IN 1ST COLUMN	4000
5 OF A KIND	200		2000
ROYAL FLUSH W/JOKER	100		1000
STRAIGHT FLUSH	50		500
4 OF A KIND	20		200
FULL HOUSE	5		50
FLUSH	3		30
STRAIGHT	3		30
3 OF A KIND	2		20
2 PAIR	1		10
KINGS OR BETTER	1		10

Joker Poker — 1 Wild Card:

Quarters & Dollars:

WINNING HAND	1 COIN	2 COINS	3 COINS	4 COINS	5 COINS
ROYAL FLUSH	400	800	1200	1600	4000/
W/O JOKER					4700
5 OF A KIND	200	400	600	800	1000
ROYAL FLUSH	100	200	300	400	500
W/JOKER					
STRAIGHT FLUSH	50	100	150	200	250
4 OF A KIND	15	30	45	60	75
FULL HOUSE	7	14	21	28	35
FLUSH	5	10	15	20	25
STRAIGHT	3	6	9	12	15
3 OF A KIND	2	4	6	8	10
2 PAIR	1	2	3	4	5
KINGS OR BETTER	1	2	3	4	5

Deuces Wild — 4 Wild Cards:

Quarters & Dollars:

WINNING HAND	1 COIN	2 COINS	3 COINS	4 COINS	5 COINS
ROYAL FLUSH	250	500	750	1000	4000/
W/O DEUCES					4700
4 DEUCES	200	400	600	800	1000
ROYAL FLUSH	25	50	75	100	125
W/DEUCES					
5 OF A KIND	15	30	45	60	75
STRAIGHT FLUSH	9	18	27	36	45
4 OF A KIND	5	10	15	20	25
FULL HOUSE	3	6	9	12	15
FLUSH	2	4	6	8	10
STRAIGHT	2	4	6	8	10
3 OF A KIND	1	2	3	4	5
2 PAIR	—	—	—	—	—
KINGS OR BETTER	—	—	—	—	—

These typical paytables for one coin played are condensed into one table for easy reference and comparison on Page 58.

Basic Rules of Strategy

Rather than trying to memorize complicated tables and charts for every possible hand, a more relaxed approach is to learn to evaluate each hand when dealt as to the best possibilities such as:

1. A Pat Hand (automatic win) that would be foolish to change.
2. A Pat Hand that has realistic chances for upgrading.
3. A so-so win that only returns your bet but can be "gambled" into a variety of possible wins.
4. A losing hand with great potential.
5. A losing hand with little or no potential.

We're going to give you seven examples of the best hands and the way to play them. A comparison of the potential return for a single coin played on three types of quarter machines will show you how to evaluate your hand and to exercise the following choices:

1. Which type of machine — Straight Poker, Joker Poker, or Deuces Wild — has the best paytables.
2. Whether you want to "play it safe" or gamble on a potential upgrade.

BEST CHOICES:
 1. **HOLD the following PAT Hands: RF, SF, 5's, 4's, AND FH.**
Example: A♡, K♡, Q♡, J♡, 10♡ = Royal Flush in Hearts

9♠, 8♠, 7♠, 6♠, 5♠ = Straight Flush in Spades

Note: A Royal Flush, Straight Flush, or Straight does not have to be shown in order on the screen (A,Q,K,10,J).

3♠, 3♡, 3♣, 3♢, & either a W2 or WJ = 5's

7♠, 7♡, 7♣, 7♢ = 4's

9♡, 9♣, 9♢, 4♠, 4♣ = FULL HOUSE

Note: Playing a Jokers Wild or Deuces Wild machine, the wild cards could stand in for any of the cards given.

2. Hold a Pat Flush unless you have four cards to a Royal Flush.

Example: A♠, Q♠, J♠, 10♠, 4♠ = FLUSH

GAMBLE: Discard the 4♠ and draw for the K♠ or a wild card.

WIN Differential:

Straight Poker	8 coins	versus	250 coins RF
Jokers Wild	5 coins	versus	100 coins RFWJ
Deuces Wild	2 coins	versus	25 coins RFW2

You are in essence "gambling" your "pat" win against a higher pot. You may also get a flush with any other card of the same suit; a straight with a king from a different suit; or, on a Straight Poker machine the possibility of Jacks or better. Any of these can give you a win or at least your money back.

3. Hold a Pat Straight unless you have four cards to a Royal Flush.

Example: K♡, Q♡, J♡, 10♡, A♠

GAMBLE: Discard the A♠ and draw for the A♡ for the RF or the 9♡ for a SF.

WIN Differential:

Straight Poker	4 coins	versus	250 coins RF

Jokers Wild	3 coins	versus	100 coins RFWJ
Deuces Wild	2 coins	versus	25 coins RFW2
Straight Poker	4 coins	versus	50 coins SF

4. Hold a Pat Straight unless you have four cards to a Straight Flush.

Example: 4♡, 5♡, 6♡, 7♡, 3♣ (Open ended ST)
      5♠, 6♠, 8♠, 9♠, 7♢ (Inside ST)

GAMBLE: Discard the 3♣ and draw for a 8♡ or a 3♡ for a SF.

          Discard the 7♢ and draw for 7♠ or a wild card.

WIN Differential:

Straight Poker	4 coins	versus	50 coins SF
Jokers Wild	3 coins	versus	50 coins SFWJ
Deuces Wild	2 coins	versus	9 coins SFW2

Note: Most strategists would stand on a Pat Straight rather than gamble as shown above, especially on an inside Straight. Take your choice, or play your hunch.

5. Hold four cards to a Straight Flush open on both ends even if you have to split a high or low pair.

Example: 3♡, 5♡, 6♡, 4♡, 6♣.
      Q♠, J♠, 10♠, 9♠, Q♢

GAMBLE: Discard the 6♣ and draw for a 2♡ or a 7♡ for a SF.

          Discard the Q♢ and draw for a 8♠, K♠, or wild card. You could also win a flush or a straight.

WIN Differential:

| Straight Poker | loser | versus | 50 coins SF |
| Jokers Wild | loser | versus | 50 coins SFWJ |

Deuces Wild	loser	versus	9 coins SFW2
Straight Poker	loser	versus	6 coins F
Jokers Wild	loser	versus	5 coins F
Deuces Wild	loser	versus	2 coins F
Straight Poker	loser	versus	4 coins S
Jokers Wild	loser	versus	3 coins S
Deuces Wild	loser	versus	2 coins S

ALTERNATE GAMBLE:

Hold the Pair of Queens or Pair of 6's

Straight Poker	loser	versus	25 coins 4's
Straight Poker	loser	versus	9 coins FH
Straight Poker	loser	versus	3 coins 3's
Straight Poker	loser	versus	2 coins 2PR
Straight Poker	QQ	wins	1 coin JB
Jokers Wild	loser	versus	250 coins 5's
Jokers Wild	loser	versus	15 coins 4's
Jokers Wild	loser	versus	7 coins FH
Jokers Wild	loser	versus	2 coins 3's
Jokers Wild	loser	versus	1 coin 2PR
Deuces Wild	loser	versus	15 coins 5's
Deuces Wild	loser	versus	5 coins 4's
Deuces Wild	loser	versus	3 coins FH
Deuces Wild	loser	versus	1 coin 3's

Note: The above possible wins are the same for a hand with any pair and miscellaneous cards to draw to.

6. Hold three of a kind (this also means a pair with a wild card). Never hold a kicker.
Example: 9♡, 9♠, 9♢, Q♢, J♠
Gamble: discard the Q♢ & J♠

Possible WINS:

Straight Poker	3 coins	for	3 of a kind
Straight Poker	3 coins	versus	25 coins 4's
Straight Poker	3 coins	versus	9 coins FH
Jokers Wild	2 coins	for	3 of a kind
Jokers Wild	2 coins	versus	200 coins 5's
Jokers Wild	2 coins	versus	15 coins 4's
Jokers Wild	2 coins	versus	7 coins FH
Deuces Wild	1 coin	for	3 of a kind
Deuces Wild	1 coin	versus	15 coins 5's
Deuces Wild	1 coin	versus	5 coins 4's
Deuces Wild	1 coin	versus	3 coins FH

7. Hold Two Pair

Example: K♠, K◇, 3♠, 3♡, 9♣

Gamble: Discard the losing 9♣, unless you're playing
          Deuces Wild, and then hold only one pair.
          (Deuces Wild do not pay on two pair.) If
          you're playing a Jokers Wild you could take
          the even money and play it safe, or gamble and
          hold only one pair for better results.

Possible WINS:

Straight Poker	2 coins	for	2 pair
Straight Poker	2 coins	versus	9 coins FH
Jokers Wild	1 coin	for	2 pair
Jokers Wild	1 coin	versus	200 coins 5's
Jokers Wild	1 coin	versus	15 coins 4's
Jokers Wild	1 coin	versus	7 coins FH
Deuces Wild	loser	versus	15 coins 5's
Deuces Wild	loser	versus	5 coins 4's
Deuces Wild	loser	versus	3 coins FH

The previous examples should help you to evaluate a hand according to the type of machine you're playing. It's easier when you're playing because the appropriate paytable is right in front of you for comparison of choices.

You can practice on basic strategies on the rest of these sample hands to determine the best choices and win differential according to the paytables we've included.

8. **Hold a High Pair and draw three cards on a Straight Poker machine, which returns your money on Jacks or Better, even if you have to break up a four-card flush or four-card straight.**

Example: J♡, 2◇, 4◇, 7◇, J◇
                 A♠, A♣, 3♠, 4♣, 5♡

9. **Hold only one of a High Pair if you have any of the following potential winners:**

Example: Four Cards to a Royal Flush
                 A◇, A♡, K◇, Q◇, J◇ (Discard A♡)
                 Four Cards to a Straight Flush (open both ends)
                 Q♡, Q♠, J♠, 10♠, 9♠ (Discard Q♡)
                 Four Cards to a Straight Flush (open one end)
                 A♠, 2♠, 3♠, 4♠, A♡ (Discard A♡)

10. **Split a low pair in favor of a Four-Card Flush.**
Example: 4◇, 4♠, 9♠, 10♠, 7♠ (Discard 4◇)

11. **Hold a low pair rather than a Four-Card Straight even if it is open ended.**
Example: 5♣, 5♠, 7♣, 6♡, 4◇ (Draw three cards)

12. Draw one card to a Four-Card open ended Straight.
Example: 3♡, 5◇, 4♠, 6♠, 9♣ (Discard 9♣)

13. Hold a High Pair or a Low Pair rather than a Three or Four-Card inside Straight.
Example: J◇, J♠, 10♣, 8♡, 7◇ (Hold JACKS)
          Q♡, Q♣, J♠, 9♣, 4◇ (Hold QUEENS)

14. Hold only one High Card unless you have two or more of the same suit for a potential Royal Flush. Otherwise hold the suit with least cards dealt.
Example: A♡, 9♣, 6♣, J◇, Q♠, (Hold A♡)
          A♡, K♡, 10♡, 6♣, 8◇ (Hold A♡, K♡, 10♡)
          K◇, J◇, 3♡, 4♡, Q♣ (Hold K◇, & J◇)

15. All other hands — get a new deal. You might be dealt a Royal Flush or other winner.

We have not given examples of all the variations that could occur. There are so many that they could fill a volume.

Common Strategic Errors that Limit Your Potential Wins

1. Holding two different high cards of different suits.
   Limits you to wins of 2PR, 3's, ST, FH, & 4's
   LOCKS OUT — F, SF, RF & 5's
2. Holding three different high cards of different suits.
   Limits you to wins of 2PR, 3's, ST
   LOCKS OUT — ALL OTHER POSSIBILITIES

3. Holding 3 low cards to an inside straight except with Joker Poker and Deuces Wild.
4. Playing too fast without seriously evaluating your hand. Speed will come with practice.

A few additional tips: Remember that large progressive jackpots for a Royal Flush almost always have a reduced payout for lower ranked hands, most often for Full Houses, Flushes, and sometimes Straights.

Study the Payout table before you insert any coins and know what to expect if you win.

Don't forget the best advice of all — "Bet with your head, not over it."

Professional Video Poker Teams

There has been some publicity about teams of professional video poker players monopolizing the banks of progressive machines. Apparently they even advertise for and pay slot players by the hour to play for them. We contacted several Las Vegas casinos to determine the extent of the problem. Most responses were that they are aware of the team players and can "handle" them.

Gary Hunter, Director of Slot Operations at the Gold Coast said these "parasites" wait until the jackpots reach a certain high figure and then try to move in. The casino bars them from tying up all the machines and does not allow them to exclude other players. According to Hunter, casinos have a right to exclude service to anyone who becomes belligerent with casino personnel.

Richard Bay, Director of Slot Operations at the Maxim, said that sometimes these teams also get "stuck" when a "non-team" player wins the big pot.

The casinos' main interest is that the machines are played as much as possible around the clock. If team players are willing to hang in during the wee hours of the morning when others are sleeping, why should the casinos object.

For that matter, not only professional players look for the biggest progressive pots. We advise that all players do the same. Always go for the biggest pot compatible with your bankroll. Remember, though, never play less than the maximum coins on progressives. Otherwise stay away from them. Don't help build a jackpot you aren't trying to win.